PRAISE FOR *DEVELOPING FEMALE LEADERS*

"In *Developing Female Leaders*, Kadi Cole gives leaders a virtual master class on women in leadership. This is a must-read for both men and women. Kadi dives into some of the most sensitive issues leaders face about men and women in the workplace with wisdom, insight, clarity, and accuracy. You'll find this book tremendously thoughtful, practical, and helpful."

—Carey Nieuwhof, founding pastor, Connexus Church;
author of *Didn't See It Coming*

"*Developing Female Leaders* is the book for this time for all leaders. Practical, well researched, honestly facing the nuances, and written in a compelling and powerful style that if followed will define the church of the future."

—Jo Anne Lyon, ambassador, general superintendent emerita
for the Wesleyan Church

"At a time when leadership is at a premium, there is a wealth of talented women ready to lead. Kadi shows us how to maximize their potential by offering readers a practical, balanced approach to equipping and empowering the next generation of female leaders."

—Jerry Hurley, team development leader, Life Church,
Oklahoma City, Oklahoma

"I first met Kadi in a roundtab' ⋯ ᶜthe largest churches in America. As t' ⋯ ʰe other
person who stood out was K ⋯ ιn in the
room that day. As a church lea ⋯ obvious
to me that the landscape of ν ⋯ ιdi's life,
her stories, and the stories of others she has gathered will inspire you."

—Pastor Joel A'Bell, lead pastor, Hillsong Church Australia

"The church has never needed women leaders more than today. Kadi Cole is bringing wise guidance to a crucial area."

—**John Ortberg**, senior pastor, Menlo Church;
author of *Eternity Is Now in Session*

"How I wish this book had been available decades ago when I began to lead in the local church! I highly recommend this tool for church leaders who know we can do better, who believe that God's best is for men and women to serve with mutual respect in healthy cultures where all of us can thrive."

—**Nancy Beach**, leadership coach, Slingshot Group; author of *Gifted to Lead: The Art of Leading as a Woman in the Church*

"Kadi Cole has provided an excellent resource that can help any organization more effectively and intentionally identify and develop what is sadly an untapped source of leadership in many Christian organizations. The last two chapters alone are worth the price of the book for any leader. Practical, insightful, and healthy, *Developing Female Leaders* is a guide you and your ministry will reference for many years to come."

—**Bill Willits**, executive director of Ministry Environments, North Point Ministries; coauthor of *Creating Community: 5 Keys to Building a Small Group Culture*

"Kadi has given us a gift that every leader needs: the tools to develop women leaders. Written with courage, honesty, and insight that comes from years of experience, *Developing Female Leaders* is a book we can't lead without."

—**Sherry Surratt**, executive director of Parent Strategies at Orange Ministries

"Kadi was one of the trailblazers for women in leadership at Christ Fellowship. We credit Kadi with helping us make God-given vision a reality around here. Every time I travel, I run across people who mention how much they admire Kadi. It makes me so proud to have supported her to be all God ordained her to be as a woman leading the way in ministry today. This book will be a game-changer for you and your team."

—**Tom Mullins**, founding pastor, Christ Fellowship Church

"This powerful book is unique, well researched, and desperately needed. I love my friend Kadi Cole's spirit in how she writes. Her candid stories and practical advice made me uncomfortable in places, but I kept reading because, frankly, I needed it. The chapter on best practices for developing female leaders is worth more than the price of the book."

—**Warren Bird, PhD**, author or coauthor of thirty-one books, including
Hero Maker, Teams That Thrive, and *How to Break Growth Barriers*

"Culture changes through conversations. Kadi Cole's *Developing Female Leaders* equips church leaders with the tools to further those conversations. Her meaningful insights gained from years of personal experience can be the catalyst for the body of Christ becoming more whole and complete."

—**Kevin Penry**, directional leader of operations 2000–2017,
Life Church, Oklahoma City, Oklahoma

"A groundbreaking resource that will become a foundational building block for churches and ministries who seek to raise up gifted female leaders. Kadi is an outstanding practitioner who offers tested leadership principles and insightful research along with very practical ideas that can be put into play immediately. You will keep this book close to your workspace and refer to it over and over again for many years to come!"

—**Jon Ferguson**, cofounder, Community Christian Church and NewThing

"Regardless of your view of the role of women in the church, this book is a helpful guide on how to relate to and develop the women leaders in your congregation. Kadi Cole addresses the stereotypes, misconceptions, and abuses that women church leaders have endured. More importantly she offers practical help in creating healthy church environments and relationships for female leaders to flourish and grow. "

—**Jim Tomberlin**, pastor, author, founder of MultiSite Solutions

"A brilliant and timely must-read for all Christian leaders regardless of your theological viewpoint. Kadi Cole brings needed clarity and practical insights that will help us better value, respect, and mobilize at least half of those who attend our churches."

—**Steve Stroope**, lead pastor, Lake Pointe Church; author of *Tribal Church*

"What a timely book for the church! This is a super practical book for women trying to find their place in leadership. And it is also a book for those who are helping women develop their leadership capacity. Get this book, read it, and unleash the potential of the women in your church!"

—**Jim Sheppard**, CEO and principal, Generis

"An extremely practical and balanced approach to taking on what can sometimes be a hot button issue. Every pastor and ministry leader who is serious about incorporating the equal gifts and holy calling of women in our churches should read, learn from, and consider these best practices."

—**Jimmy Scroggins**, lead pastor, Family Church

DEVELOPING
female
LEADERS

DEVELOPING
female
LEADERS

NAVIGATE THE MINEFIELDS AND RELEASE
*THE **POTENTIAL OF WOMEN** IN YOUR CHURCH*

KADI COLE

THOMAS NELSON
Since 1798

Published in Nashville, Tennessee, by Thomas Nelson. Thomas Nelson is a registered trademark of HarperCollins Christian Publishing, Inc.

Thomas Nelson titles may be purchased in bulk for educational, business, fund-raising, or sales promotional use. For information, please e-mail SpecialMarkets@ThomasNelson.com.

Unless otherwise noted, Scripture quotations are taken from the Holy Bible, New International Version®, NIV®. Copyright © 1973, 1978, 1984, 2011 by Biblica, Inc.® Used by permission of Zondervan. All rights reserved worldwide. www.Zondervan.com. The "NIV" and "New International Version" are trademarks registered in the United States Patent and Trademark Office by Biblica, Inc.®

Scripture quotations marked NKJV are from the New King James Version®. © 1982 by Thomas Nelson. Used by permission. All rights reserved.

Any Internet addresses, phone numbers, or company or product information printed in this book are offered as a resource and are not intended in any way to be or to imply an endorsement by Thomas Nelson, nor does Thomas Nelson vouch for the existence, content, or services of these sites, phone numbers, companies, or products beyond the life of this book.

ISBN 978-1-4002-1093-0 (eBook)
ISBN 978-1-4002-1092-3 (TP)

Library of Congress Control Number: 2018956698

Printed in the United States of America

19 20 21 22 23 LSC 10 9 8 7 6 5 4 3 2 1

About Leadership ✳ Network

Leadership Network fosters innovation movements that activate the church to greater impact. We help shape the conversations and practices of pacesetter churches in North America and around the world. The Leadership Network mind-set identifies church leaders with forward-thinking ideas—and helps them to catalyze those ideas resulting in movements that shape the church.

Together with HarperCollins Christian Publishing, the biggest name in Christian books, the NEXT imprint of Leadership Network moves ideas to implementation for leaders to take their ideas to form, substance, and reality. Placed in the hands of other church leaders, that reality begins spreading from one leader to the next . . . and to the next . . . and to the next, where that idea begins to flourish into a full-grown movement that creates a real, tangible impact in the world around it.

NEXT: A Leadership Network Resource
committed to helping you grow your next idea.

LEADERSHIP NETWORK

leadnet.org/NEXT

This book is dedicated to
The women who modeled godly female leadership for me . . .
My mom, Harriet. You are one of my richest blessings.
My spiritual leadership mentor and lifelong friend, Jill Brandenburg.
My favorite kick-butt female boss, Dr. Marianne May.
And the men who went out of their way to
open leadership doors for me . . .
Pastor Gale Fister, Jim Kuffel, Bob Woods, Dr. Doug
Randlett, Pastor Jeff Bogue, Pastor Todd Mullins,
and Greg Ligon. There are no words.

CONTENTS

WELCOME

"You have really nice birthing hips."

That was my introduction to ministry leadership as a female. I had recently moved across the country for my first job after college and was volunteering to lead the name tag table for my church's singles ministry picnic. I was energetic, naive, hopeful, and ready to share Jesus' love with everyone I met. That creepy forty-five-year-old divorcé took me completely by surprise.

I had no idea what to do. Was he joking? Did I somehow send a wrong signal? What is the right way to respond to this?

I awkwardly tried to laugh it off in the moment, but I've never forgotten how suddenly out of place and vulnerable I felt. Thankfully, I had some great leaders who came beside me, rolled their eyes with me, and helped me find other avenues and experiences that were the exact opposite—affirming, uplifting, and a whole lot of fun. Had they not, I am pretty sure the "birthing hips" guy and a handful of other unfortunate encounters would have derailed my passion for serving in ministry and eroded my trust in the people who make up Jesus' church. Oh, how much I would have missed out on.

I am not the only one with these kinds of stories. In fact, the more female ministry leaders I meet, the more incredible stories I hear. Some are hilarious, some are ridiculous, and some will make you cry. There is great power in remembering and sharing our experiences—especially for young leaders coming behind us.

Some amazing leaders (both male and female) did that for me, so this book is my attempt to get powerful stories to more churches, more leadership teams, and more up-and-coming female leaders to encourage, inspire, and challenge all of us to fully fulfill our callings.

I realize that females in church leadership is a controversial topic, and although I am not normally one to engage in such an emotionally charged debate, this one continues to bubble up in almost every conversation or leadership engagement I have. Because I come from a spiritually rich and eclectic Christian church background, I have grown to love, understand, and appreciate people and ministries on all sides of this theological issue.

I grew up in the mountains of Montana, where gender roles are not very traditional—men often cook and garden, while women frequently hunt and know how to change their own oil. But most of the women I saw in our small mission church served only in traditional female roles, such as in the nursery and the kitchen. In college I was part of a Lutheran church near Seattle where women were fully ordained and no one ever gave it a second thought. I have been part of a Baptist church in the South where I watched a highly educated female staff member consistently hesitate in giving her full perspective to the senior pastor, even though he asked for her honest opinion. And I have been on leadership staff at a church that started out on one side of this issue and transitioned to the other side. They were all wonderful places to grow, contribute, learn, and lead.

Now, in my work as a church consultant and leadership coach, I get to see God working in a lot of different contexts and approaches. I love them all, and I honestly respect everyone's view on this issue. But something has shifted recently in my work with church leaders.

Usually when I speak at a conference or lead a training at a church, it is the female leaders who are excited to connect and talk about my personal journey, especially how I ended up leading at high levels in churches that were not publicly open to having women in positions of leadership. But more and more lately, I have been approached by male senior pastors and executive leaders asking me questions about what they can do to help develop the young female leaders on their staffs and in their congregations. I talk about pipelines and trainings, getting women leaders out of administrative/secretarial titles, and how to cast vision and provide clarity about the issue with their teams.

As we talk, they will typically nod and take notes. Usually they will have a couple of follow-up questions, and sometimes offer a description of the existing women on their team and an explanation of what they have done so far to help them grow as leaders. That's when it will get weird. I actually hear things like:

- "I promoted her to my assistant so she can sit in on the executive team meetings."
- "I assume we will only have her for a couple more years until she starts having kids."
- "I asked my wife (who does not work at the church) to start mentoring her."
- "She comes on a little strong, which makes our team nervous."
- "I talked with her husband to see if she'd be willing to increase her hours."
- "I didn't want her to feel awkward being the only girl, so we didn't bring her."
- "We have a big women's ministry, so she gets what she needs spiritually there."
- "We were going to give her a promotion, but she became pregnant, and we didn't want to overload her with a baby on the way."

It always takes me by surprise. These are really amazing men—the highest-level leaders in their churches. They are intelligent, love the Lord, have great people skills, and are trying like crazy to make a way for the female talent they see on their teams.

But here's what I have come to realize: they meant well, but they simply did not know what they did not know. I am calling it "lovingly ignorant." How could these leaders be expected to do things differently if they did not understand *why* these perspectives and actions are not helpful?

That is why I wrote this book. I hope to highlight the issues and help church leaders think more critically about what they believe and how they can be even more intentional about elevating and empowering the female leaders serving on their teams and sitting in their congregations.

Throughout this book you will find a collection of stories, experiences, research, interviews, perspectives, advice, warnings, wisdom, and candor gleaned from

- more than thirty executive and high-level female ministry leaders in a variety of settings, including some of the world's biggest and most influential churches;
- more than one thousand female leaders from churches across America and in several other countries who completed our survey about developing female leaders; and
- a handful of brave male leaders from some of America's most influential churches who are actively engaging this issue and seeing the fruit of releasing women to contribute their all in ministry.

There are discussion questions at the end of the book that you can work through by yourself or together with your leadership team.

My only intent is to help. If you are someone who is open, curious, hungry, passionate, or perhaps even determined to move this topic forward in your church, I pray this book will serve as a conversation catalyst, a useful tool to help you make changes, and a source of encouragement and inspiration for "what could be."

FOR CHURCH LEADERS

I hope you will begin to see the talented, gifted, and anointed women God has brought to your church in a new light. I pray you will catch the vision God has for how you are to equip and empower their dormant potential so your whole church might benefit from their impact and fulfill the mission you have been called to lead.

FOR WOMEN EARLY IN THEIR LEADERSHIP JOURNEY (REGARDLESS OF YOUR AGE)

I hope you learn from these storytellers and wisdom-givers. Be inspired by their courage, tenacity, mistakes, victories, calling, and sanctification. I pray you begin to see your potential and your pathway more clearly, as God sees it.

FOR SEASONED FEMALE LEADERS

I hope this book is a confirmation that your faithfulness and presence in ministry makes a difference. It matters that you keep showing up. It matters that you keep learning and growing. And it matters that you begin to raise the dialog, educate the leaders around you, invest in the younger female leaders coming after you, and leave things better than you found them. You matter.

The positive evidence for diversity of all kinds on our teams and in our workplaces has been clear for a long time: higher productivity, enhanced culture, increased talent retention, more innovation and creativity, greater social impact, and improved leadership decision making.[1] And that's just in the business world. What could our churches be like if we got better in all these areas? What kind of impact could we see for the kingdom if we embraced the power of diversity?

I hope we get to find out.

Best Practice #1

1

SEEK TO UNDERSTAND

W here are all the ladies?" asked Pastor Joel A'Bell, the lead pastor of Hillsong Church Australia. Everyone looked around the room sheepishly. A couple of leaders chuckled under their breath. I tried to smile politely but avoided eye contact with anyone.

This wasn't the first room of church leaders in which I was the only female. Nor was it the biggest. But it was, hands down, the most intimidating. And it had nothing to do with being a woman.

This was the annual gathering of executive pastors of large multisite churches. They had met through a Leadership Network[1] community in the early 2000s, when multisite was a brand-new concept, and no one had yet heard the term *campus pastor* or was using a matrix organizational structure in a church. They continue to meet every year to learn from one another, share what they are working on, and encourage one another in the work of ministry around the globe.

That year my home church was hosting it, and my executive pastor, who was recruiting me to come back on staff as part of the executive team, had invited me to join in for a few days to "get a taste of what I would be a part of." (Not a bad recruiting strategy, right?)

Pastor Joel eyed the room as if he actually wanted an answer. Being from another country and working in ministries around the world, he was not used to this kind of homogeny. What seemed "normal" to us raised a red flag to him. None of us had any good answers, especially me. I was just thankful to be in the room.

Another male executive pastor put it this way: "There are all these talented women in our congregation, but it's like they can't break through, even as volunteers. We want them to, but we just can't seem to figure it out. I come from the corporate world, and this is just baffling to me."

Baffling is a good word for it. It can be confusing for pastors who are open to women doing more in their churches but find there is this invisible barrier to recruiting and retaining high-quality female leaders.

What is it? If we clearly have needs that a female leader could fill and we have qualified women available, what is the holdup?

To answer that question, you have to get a little inside a woman's head. I know that's a scary thought, but bear with me. If you want to understand the holdup, you must understand the pushback. You have to learn what many of the women in your congregation are battling internally so you can encourage and challenge them in the right ways.

Obviously, every woman is different. But following are the most common challenges or paradoxes that the women we interviewed and surveyed are facing. I encourage you to ask some of the women leaders on your team and in your congregation for their experiences and perspectives around these concepts. You may find that many of them are true and the learning will be worth it. Without a deeper understanding, you will stay baffled, and they will stay underutilized.

CONDITIONING

As I have talked with male leaders about this subject, it has been hard for me to find the adequate words to describe the effects that many cultures have on a woman's view of herself, her role, her calling, and her potential. Many things influence this during our growing-up years—our family dynamics, the area of the country in which we lived, the type of school we attended, and the culture of our church. Most women who are over thirty-five likely grew up with parents of the Boomer generation (born between 1946 and 1964), in which gender roles were clear but were being challenged in progressive ways. If they grew up in the church, however, these traditional gender roles stayed strongly in place for another twenty or thirty years.

Now, I love being a woman, and I really love the men in my life. I would not want any of us to give up our gender identities or the God-ordained uniquenesses they express. So when I'm talking about gender roles, I am not talking about actual gender or the beauty that God reveals in men and women. But I am talking about the stereotypical roles we easily assign to people based solely on gender. Things like these:

- Men are better at science, technology, finance, problem-solving, and video games. All men enjoy working on cars, fixing things around the house, politics, sports, and outdoor activities like fishing and hunting. Men are sloppy, lazy, and do not cook or clean. All men are competitive and natural leaders.
- Women are naturally talented at teaching, organizing, cooking, cleaning, and relationships. All women enjoy kids, fashion, spending money, decorating, shopping, and dancing. Women are neither technical nor able to fix things such as cars or household appliances. Women avoid physically demanding work and

prefer not to sweat. Women are relational peacemakers and natural followers.

Each of us has grown up connecting with some of the stereotypes of our gender and some that do not fit us at all. I know many men who feel insecure that they aren't good at sports or that they can't fix things around the house. What a shame! God hand-makes each one of us and gives us a unique style to fit our specific calling. Stereotypes hurt everyone. Wherever she adopted hers, the effects of these messages over decades greatly influence what a developing female leader thinks about herself, how she can please God, and what she can offer in service at her church.

The best way I know to describe it to someone who has not experienced her gender be a leadership liability is to flip the table on the guys. To get a better understanding of what this would feel like, the following is a spoof on gender equality that I first heard at a conference for higher-education professionals. This is not meant to be insulting to anyone's theological position, but I do want to challenge you to think about how you would view your leadership capacity differently if this is what you heard on a weekly basis during your formative growing-up years.

10 Reasons Why Men Shouldn't Be Pastors, by David Scholer[2]

10. A man's place is in the army.
9. For men who have children, their duties might distract them from the responsibility of being a parent.
8. Their physical build indicates that they are more suited to such tasks as chopping down trees and wrestling mountain lions. It would be "unnatural" for them to do other forms of work.

7. Man was created before woman, obviously as a prototype. Thus, men represent an experiment, rather than the crowning achievement of creation.

6. Men are too emotional to be priests or pastors. Their conduct at football and basketball games demonstrates this.

5. Some men are handsome, and this will distract women worshippers.

4. Pastors need to nurture their congregations. But this is not a traditional male role. Throughout history, women have been recognized as not only more skilled than men at nurturing but also more fervently attracted to it. This makes them the obvious choice for ordination.

3. Men are overly prone to violence. No "manly man" wants to settle disputes by any means other than by fighting about it. Thus, they would be poor role models, as well as being dangerously unstable in positions of leadership.

2. The New Testament tells us that Jesus was betrayed by a man. His lack of faith and ensuing punishment remind us of the subordinated position that men should take.

1. Men can still be involved in church activities, even without being ordained. They can sweep sidewalks, repair the church roof, and perhaps even lead the singing on Father's Day. By confining themselves to such traditional male roles, they can still be vitally important in the life of the church.

Crazy, right? To think of sending young men these messages goes against everything we have been taught. Yet women receive these messages all the time.

- A woman's place is in the home.
- Women are physically and mentally designed primarily for childbearing.

- Women are highly emotional and have a hard time making clear decisions or communicating effectively.
- Women, especially beautiful ones, are a temptation to men and cannot be trusted to maintain appropriate boundaries.
- Women are secondary and find their value through the men in their lives.

For a young female leader, these subtle (and sometimes not-so-subtle) messages can really wreak havoc on her understanding of who God has made her to be and what He has called her to do.

However, if she grew up in a home that did not live out strong gender-stereotyped roles, chances are she did not absorb the message quite as strongly as those who did. In fact, one of the most surprising findings in our interviews is that, of the thirty high-level female ministry leaders we interviewed, almost all of them grew up without traditional gender-typed females. For example, either both of the leader's parents worked full-time with successful careers, or she grew up with a single mom whom she saw do all aspects of home life, house maintenance, and parenting, or she attended an all-girls school in which young women filled all roles in sports, student government, and academics, including science, technology, math, and engineering. This seems to have built up their leadership skills and confidence in two ways:

- These women didn't know they should not pursue a job or role that seemed interesting to them. They watched leaders around them, and rather than seeing gender, they saw gifting, passion, and abilities. These were the items they used as the basis for deciding if the role would be a good fit for them or not. The question was never, "Will I be allowed?"; it was always, "Do I want to try this?" or "Is this a good fit for me?"
- Since many of these women jumped into male-dominated

environments in school or work early on, they learned how to build relationships, navigate the challenges, and grow a "thick skin" that was incredibly useful for leading in a church led mostly by men. One woman commented that it was so much easier to grow in a male-dominated environment because her leaders and peers were "straight shooters," consistently giving her clear and real-time feedback on how she could improve. Almost all the interviewees could see this now in retrospect, but at the time they had no idea how God was preparing them for ministry leadership.

Could it be that this "first generation" of female executive-level ministry leaders had a possible advantage because their formative years gave them permission to live beyond gender stereotypes? Perhaps they were able to break through the glass ceiling in churches—often called the "stained glass ceiling"[3]—because in the foundation of who they saw themselves to be, there was no assumed limitation to what they could do. To me, this has two big implications:

- This next generation of women, who have grown up with a much more expanded view of what a woman is capable of, will bring with them a level of skill and confidence that we have never seen in the church. Think of the potential they have and what we would be missing out on if they only found a place for their leadership skills outside the church. Figuring out how to develop these leaders and empower them for ministry could not be more important, or more urgent!
- Our early discipleship programs (pre–high school) need to include intentional gender-based programming in which little girls and boys get to experience and experiment with all the roles it takes to become and make disciples. They need to see lots of examples of both men and women filling various ministry roles

based on their giftedness, not just on their gender. There needs not only to be freedom for men to be greeters and women to be ushers, but for men to be behind-the-scenes in the kitchen and women to be up front and onstage. The earlier this starts, the better opportunity we have to support our congregation in discovering and fulfilling their God-given purpose.

In addition to the individual messages a female leader has been given, we also have to remember the bigger American cultural limitations women have faced. Although these aren't necessarily a part of daily life for all women now, our mothers and grandmothers (who greatly influence our thinking about our potential as women) grew up in a very different world. Here's a little perspective on where we have come from as a nation around the equality of women in the last one hundred years.

- Before 1920 a woman could not vote in America.[4]
- Before 1963 it was legal to pay a woman less than a man for equal work (at the time women were paid 41 percent less in the same job).[5]
- Before 1974 a women could not apply for a credit card without a husband or father as a cosigner.[6]
- Before 1975 there were states where women could not serve on juries.[7]
- Before 1978 a woman could lose her job for becoming pregnant.[8]
- Before 1980 there was no definition for sexual harassment and therefore no way for a woman to be protected, especially in her workplace.[9]

My mom has been my biggest cheerleader, but she grew up in a time when women were treated very differently than men. Her mother had not been allowed to vote as a young adult. My mom was paid significantly less than her male peers and could not have her own credit card until her late thirties. She is the first woman in her family to go to college, but thought her only options were to become a teacher or a nurse. And she lived through decades of unprotested sexual harassment.

So it should be no surprise that when I took big steps toward independence or leadership, my mom, although trying to be supportive, was also very concerned. She didn't want me to be disappointed. She didn't want me to fail. She didn't want me to hit the glass ceiling and be surprised. This kind of concern can sometimes feel unsupportive or as if it is questioning a young woman's ability, which isn't the case at all—a concerned mom is questioning the *world's* willingness to accept a young woman with leadership abilities.

Another way a woman can be conditioned against leading in the church are the often unnoticed, but strong statements about being female that are residual from our society's history.

I heard Julie Roys interview a young woman named Abby Snow on her Moody Bible Radio podcast *Up for Debate*. For Abby, this social conditioning showed up in a seminary class.

I remember being in a [graduate] class and we had read this book with wonderful truths, written by a godly man, but every single example about what not to do in leadership was a feminine metaphor.

It was the "nagging wife."

It was an "old wives' tale."

It was the "mother hen."

So I brought it up in class and I said, "You know, I see these biblical truths and I want to accept them with humility and wisdom, but it's very hard for me to see myself as a leader when all the negative examples about what you don't want to do in leadership

[are] feminine." So I brought this up to my professor and he's a good man and he said, "Oh, I never noticed that."[10]

Danielle, a young female community pastor, described her experiences with gender roles to me like this:

I had a couple early experiences where either a teacher or a coach or someone like that in school would call me up or place me in some sort of position of authority over my classmates, but without a title or anything, just, "Will you take care of this?" or "Will you explain this to that group of people?" I'm guessing they saw ability in me, but at the time it was very awkward and uncomfortable. "Why would you expose me like that in front of my friends who don't really want me to take charge or lead them in any way?" I can see now that they saw something in me or a certain skill set, but I didn't necessarily have a warm association with my gifting in the beginning. And then, on top of that, everything I had seen in my life thus far, when it came to gender and leadership, fell into two frameworks.

One was that I had a lot of females in my life, whether it be my mother or my grandmother or even people at church, whose gifts seemed to be beautifully demonstrated in gifts like mercy and hospitality and helps. And here they were flourishing in their gifts, and I could clearly see the mark of God on their lives. But when I tried to associate with that, it didn't feel like it fit. So I was like, "Oh well. I mean, helping people is nice, but I don't necessarily feel like I'm running in my lane." But because all the females in my life are doing this, I thought that was what femininity looked like.

But on the other side, I had male leaders in my life, including my father, who, I now recognize, had a gifting actually quite similar to mine—a gift of leadership or gift of wisdom or teaching. But I really only saw men, in my early stages, operating in these gifts, so I thought these gifts were masculine. So there was this confusion of what good femininity or masculinity were. But, in reality, it was seeing what my gifts and calling are and how that plays out in different genders. So I spent a lot of years not necessarily thinking that I was much of anything or a very good female or a very good leader.[11]

These experiences are not unique. If the women in your church are hesitant to step into higher leadership roles, accept a specific title, or take a seat at the table, there's a good reason. As you come alongside a woman, ask questions, listen, and learn about her unique viewpoint, you'll be able to uncover any misconceptions that are holding her back. You also hold incredible power to help her see herself differently, realize the potential that she does have, and open doors of opportunity that she might not otherwise know exist for her.

STICKY FLOORS

Remember that executive pastor roundtable where I was just thankful to be in the room? I look back at that now and have to laugh at myself. I made all the classic mistakes a female leader tends to make that hold herself back, often unknowingly.

- I was cautious about speaking up in any of the formal conversations. I remember sliding notes to my pastor with points written on them so he could add them to the dialogue. I even whispered a joke to him that, when he delivered it, got a big laugh from the whole room. (He graciously tried to give me credit, but somehow that never really works.) The one time I did offer my thoughts myself, I raised my hand and asked if I could say something. Why did I not think that my experience and perspective could stand on its own? Why did I assume I didn't belong there? Later I learned that I actually had as much multisite experience as many in that room, sometimes more, but at the time I couldn't even fathom that idea. I walked in assuming I knew less and had less to offer.

- I was intimidated by the leaders in the room and found it awkward to strike up any sort of personal connection. What in the world could we have in common outside of work? Plus, I had learned how cautious ministry leaders are when it comes to male-female interactions, so I waited for someone to talk to me. Why did I allow myself to miss out on these world-class leaders?

- When there was a lull between sessions and I was unsure what to do, I started picking up dirty plates and empty cups from the tables. Why did I not feel I could simply walk up and join in on one of the coffee-break conversations going on around me?

- When asked what I did in ministry, I fumbled over an explanation. How do I explain my "girl title" without droning on? Do I just re-create a title so that they understand what I do, hoping this isn't really lying? Why had I not spent any time figuring this out beforehand?

- And, of course, I was overly concerned with how I looked and the image I was projecting. Perfectionistic tendencies get in the way all the time for women, especially when it comes to appearances. We are conditioned to believe this is where much of our worth is derived. Why couldn't I just be confident in myself and authentically connect with these fellow leaders? Did they actually care about (or even notice) what I was wearing?

These and several other tendencies women have of holding themselves back from growing into leadership have become known as the "sticky floor."[12] The glass ceiling is one thing, but the sticky floor is often just as limiting, especially in ministry circles. These are the attitudes and learned behaviors that women do *to themselves* that keep them from growing in their leadership abilities and opportunities for advancement. Some "sticky floor" challenges that often hold women back include not leveraging mentoring relationships, not learning how to present themselves effectively, waiting for their hard work to be recognized by someone else rather than confidently articulating it for themselves, and not knowing how to confidently negotiate for their own value (such as schedule, salary, and benefits).[13]

Insecurities also play out in many unfortunate ways for female leaders that are helpful for you, as an organizational leader, to know. For example, if there is a job opening available, research has shown that a man will apply for that job if he is 60 percent confident that he can perform the job well. He knows he can likely figure out the other 40 percent as he goes. On the other hand, if a woman looks at a potential job opening, she will wait until she is 100 percent sure that she can perform the job well *even before applying.*[14] This has a double impact: not only does a woman miss out on opportunities to grow and become better, but her leaders never know she is interested in advancing in the organization.

It's not uncommon for me to hear from church leaders that they have job openings and have told their team that the role is open to both men and women, only to have no women apply. For most men, this seems like a mystery, and unfortunately it's easy to assume that women aren't interested in that type of role. But if you know about the 60/100 tendency, you can talk to your up-and-coming female leader about what new opportunities are available to her and why you think she would be a good fit. You can clearly explain that you don't expect her to be perfect from day one, but over the course of six months or a year you will be training her, giving her feedback, and allowing her to grow into the job. She may need more encouragement and even a little "loving push" to go for a new opportunity, but as she grows in her abilities, gains confidence, and experiences successfully growing into a position, she will be less hesitant next time.

Here are some other "sticky floor" tendencies that limit women's leadership success:[15]

- Women will often use softer words that minimize their impact ("I feel" instead of "I think" or "I know"). This can inadvertently communicate that they aren't sure if what they are saying is accurate or not.
- They'll apologize for having an opinion or for something that happened that wasn't their fault. ("I'm sorry, but I don't think your calculations are correct.")
- Women often ask for permission to give their opinions or perspectives, even if they have a clear seat at the table. This sends a message to others, and themselves, that they are not really supposed to be there.
- Self-deprecation can be a helpful tool for a strong leader, but women tend to use it more often and in more personal ways. This can communicate a lack of self-respect or an inability to see your own strengths. Playing helpless to ease the insecurity of a male leader may help you in the short term, but it simultaneously discredits the male leader's view of you in the long term.
- Women often automatically shy away from seeking out opportunities or will even turn down an invitation because they are not sure if they can deliver without failing on another responsibility. Many women need to be coached in how to lead at a *higher* level, not just add more to their already full plate.
- Although women tend to set a lot of goals for themselves, they are often either too realistic or completely unrealistic. Neither accomplishes what a healthy goal should: to stretch you to do

and be more than you think you can, without setting yourself up for failure.

- Because there is a pressure to "do it all," women often don't think about asking for help—even if they clearly need additional resources or staff to help them meet their responsibilities. This is exacerbated in the ministry and nonprofit sectors, where budgets are often tight, resources are scarce, and women feel they should just be thankful to be a part of the work.

If you keep these tendencies in mind, church leaders have an incredible opportunity to challenge and encourage women leaders to communicate more accurately in meetings, to extend a personal invitation to a woman leader to apply for a promotion by explaining why you think she can do the job, and to help her problem solve how to take on new opportunities without dropping any of the balls she is already juggling. You also can be ready to give her extra resources or take something off her plate that she likely wouldn't ask for on her own.

HOW CAN YOU LEARN MORE?

The key to this issue is to "seek to understand" on an individual basis. Take the time to have a conversation with the female leaders you have on your team and in your congregation. Ask them about their stories and how they have impacted their view of themselves as leaders.

Learn about their experiences at your church by asking intentional questions such as these and listening closely.

- Have you ever tried to lead anything at our church?
- Do you enjoy leading here? Why?

- What opportunities do you think are available to you?
- What roadblocks have you come up against when you've tried to lead?
- How does your own internal thinking impact what you lead?
- How can we, as pastors and church leaders, support you in your leadership?

On more than one interview, the female leaders we talked to emphasized the need for men to listen well. In fact, three of them said it in almost the exact same way: "Men need to ask questions and then listen . . . *really* listen." This is the first and best place to start.

The beautiful part of being in that intimidating room of executive leaders was that two executive pastors sought me out, engaged me in conversation, asked my perspective, included me in chitchat, and were complete gentlemen. I did take the job and got to spend the next six years meeting regularly with these incredible leaders, seeing more women join the group, and several of these original leaders graciously allowed me to interview them for this book. I'll be forever thankful for the time they took to reach out, get to know me, understand my story, and continue to cheer me on in personal and practical ways.

Best Practice #2

CLEARLY DEFINE WHAT
YOU BELIEVE

*I know you think you understand what you thought I
said, but I'm not sure you realize that what you heard
is not what I meant.*
—ROBERT J. MCCLOSKEY, AMERICAN DIPLOMAT (1922–1996)

I f I could choose one word to describe what it is like to be a female
leader in most ministries, it's *confusing.* Every leader faces issues of
clarity—Where are we going? Who's really in charge? How are we
getting there? What should I be doing to help?—and the most effective organizations are intentional about consistently bringing clarity
and focus to their vision, mission, and strategy. But for a woman
who is trying to lead in a church setting, these issues of clarity are
often compounded by mixed messages about what, how, and whom
she is allowed to lead.

I want to again emphasize that I fully support whatever your theological beliefs are and where you draw the line around the issue of a woman leading in your church. I can understand, appreciate, and have been a part of almost every belief system on the spectrum. What I do want to call out, however, is the space between what your theology will allow a woman to do in your church and what she *thinks* she is allowed to do. Even if you have confidence that your stance is extremely clear, there have likely been mixed messages in how this has played out for her in your church and in her leadership. In my experience, most godly women are very aware there is a line somewhere, and because they are concerned about overstepping that line, they will often stay way below what you believe they have an opportunity to do. This gap is one of the places where you have incredible untapped leadership potential.

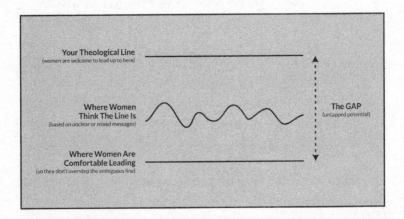

For example, let's say a church would welcome a woman to lead the greeter team since this is a highly functional role and doesn't require any biblical teaching or direct spiritual authority. This involves coordinating the schedule to make sure all the doors are covered at every service time, ordering name tags, recruiting and building the team, and helping volunteers learn the job and perform it well. However, it is also clear that women are not allowed in all roles of church leadership. There are no women on the pastoral staff, and there are rarely women leading or teaching during a weekend service.

It would not be unusual for a woman in your congregation to assume leading the greeter team is not open to her because (1) she will likely have to teach a volunteer orientation class that will include men, and (2) she may have to redirect someone doing the job incorrectly, and if this happened to be a man, she wouldn't be able to do that. If the line isn't clear or this opportunity isn't overtly communicated as being open to her as a female, it would be easy for her to assume she should not offer to serve in this role. And as we talked about in the last chapter, because most women won't feel confident enough in their abilities to apply for a leadership role they've never done before, this church is really missing out and probably doesn't even realize it.

This lack of clarity can also be a challenge for women leading in children's or student ministries, even though leading in these areas is almost never a theological controversy. But if she is trying to "stay below the line," what happens when a man joins the volunteer team? She knows it's okay to lead children, but can she lead one of their dads if he is in charge of game time?

Several male pastors I've worked with have worried that bringing clarity to this issue may send an unintended message that they are limiting a woman's potential, but in many cases, you will actually be expanding it as women realize they were leading below what is open to them.

It also brings clarity to the men of your church to know where they also can volunteer and lead if a woman has a place of leadership. If a woman cannot lead a man in any way, then men should not volunteer for children's ministry or summer camp if a woman is one of the leaders. However, if there are functional teams that do not involve preaching, for example, then men are free to be on the team and be led by a woman. For many of you this might sound crazy to have to clarify, but as I've learned more about how well-meaning church members live in ambiguity, I've discovered there is *a lot* of sideways time and energy wasted on these types of wonderings.

Northpoint Community Church's executive director of Ministry Environments, Bill Willits, explained:

> There have always been amazing women leaders, but they haven't always been available to the church. I think part of that is because they didn't know they had the opportunity. We hired a lot of part-time people when we first got started because we just didn't have the cash or the capacity to hire our full-time players. And I would say in twenty years, the volume of women leaders who are open to church ministry has skyrocketed. But twenty years ago, it was not a cultural norm, nor did we clarify the opportunities that were available.[1]

Even if your church hasn't drawn a clear line because you aren't sure where you land on this issue, I want to encourage you that simply bringing clarity (even if it is a slightly lower bar for women than you are completely comfortable with) is actually going to open up doors of opportunity for women that currently feel closed. And you still gain a lot of leadership potential!

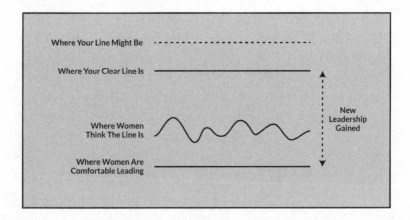

Clearly articulating your beliefs is one half of bringing clarity to this issue; the second half is aligning your practices with what you believe. To have clarity, and therefore confident and productive leaders, what your church says you believe and what your church does with those beliefs have to match.

For example, we had many women in our survey discuss that females are allowed to lead in their churches, but there are very few female leaders on the ministry staff and usually none in higher-level leadership positions.[2] It made them question whether this was really the belief system of the leaders or was "just for show."

We also had women discuss that female leaders are allowed to exercise their leadership gifts in certain ministry areas but not in others, but they were unclear why or which ones were "approved." Another area of confusion centered on pastors' wives being allowed to lead in ministry settings but not women who were single or married to someone not on the paid church staff.

The distinction between "leadership" and "spiritual authority" often needs to be clarified. Can a woman lead a five-minute devotional at the start of a team meeting? Is she allowed to pray, or does she need to ask a man in the room to pray instead?

ALIGNMENT

The alignment of beliefs and actions also communicates loudly when there are exceptions made. Many of our high-level female leaders who were interviewed started in ministry in more conservative environments, but there were unique circumstances that allowed them to lead in ways that normally wouldn't have been open to them.

One woman spent a lot of time in her early twenties participating in missionary work overseas. In these environments, women are often allowed to lead and teach men on the mission field, even though they wouldn't be allowed to do so back home. Another common environment where women are in leadership positions is in a church plant or a fast-growing ministry where trusted leaders are in high demand. Although all the women were very thankful for the opportunities these exceptions brought, their experience was often tainted with a fear that they were doing something wrong or they were confused as to why their gifts were not welcome later, when the "crisis" was over. They also encountered a lot of resistance from other women who had not had similar opportunities to lead.

It was also a common experience for many of our survey participants to organize, create, and lead basically all parts of a ministry or a project except the public leadership moments, such as opening the meeting, closing in prayer, or being publicly recognized as "the leader." In one such example, a female choir director was allowed to choose the music, decide who would sing, run the rehearsal, and direct the performance, but she wasn't allowed to turn around and face the congregation during the song performance. That would have been "leading" in that setting, and it wasn't allowed.[3] But apparently everything else she did was *not* considered leading.

Bringing "clarity" does not necessarily mean you have to jump to writing long white papers on the subject or having big, public discussions or debates. Although I know strong churches that have done that and it has been very helpful to them, I also know several equally effective churches that have their position clear in the minds of the leadership and within their culture, but have chosen not to make it a separate "written policy."

Perhaps just tweaking the language of your already existing documents is all that needs to happen to clarify your position. Any changes need to be implemented within the style of your church's culture, but the measurement of success will be that your leaders and the majority of your church members understand your beliefs in the same way, and that what they see in the leadership ranks of your church matches what you say you believe.

If you are diving into this issue for the first time, I highly recommend you give yourself the time you need to do a thorough theological study, read the many resources available on all the different viewpoints, and bathe the process in prayer for God's clear guidance and unity among the leaders involved. There is no need to rush the process in either discernment and study or in communication and implementation of any changes. However, if you already know where your theological position is, the next step is to assess how well your teams and culture are doing in being consistent with those beliefs. The more aligned your beliefs are with your practices, the clearer and more empowered your female leaders will be to maximize their potential within your ministry.

One final thought: don't be afraid to live out your convictions that are clearly based on Scripture, even if it creates some conflict and uncomfortable moments, as God will honor that. But it is important to stay attuned to your current church and community cultures. We are often called to be countercultural, but leading change well is a part of that process. Bring clarity to what you are comfortable doing, and reserve the right to update it later as you continue to study, pray, and discern more clearly what God has for your church and the people you are called to serve.

To help facilitate the assessment of your church's clarity around your theological position and culture, I've outlined a range of viewpoints on the topic of women leading in the church. Although this is certainly not exhaustive and doesn't reflect any one side's complete perspective, I hope it will provide you with an overview of the various ways this tends to be lived out in day-to-day ministry life, based on my experiences and research.

DIFFERENT VIEWS OF WOMEN
IN CHURCH LEADERSHIP

If you are new to the theological debate behind gender roles in church leadership, there are many different viewpoints, and it is a highly charged and often deeply personal topic. Because my background has included wonderful experiences in a variety of theological settings, I've been exposed to many different opinions. I highly recommend doing your own study of Scripture and reading a variety of perspectives as you wrestle with this subject with the Lord for yourself.

However, the most helpful angle for me to understand why this issue is so controversial and how such committed and biblically focused Christ-followers could see this so differently was to learn about the connection of this issue to one's understanding of how we see God and how we are made in His image. More specifically, how the Father, Son, and Holy Spirit (the Trinity) interact with one another, and how this informs how we, as God's children, should interact with one another.

Please note there are critics of using Trinitarian theology as the basis for the gender-role debate, and I respect their points. This is simply the perspective that has helped me understand the issue the most, and it gives a strong case for why the issue continues to be so hard to resolve (understanding the Trinity will always be a mystery) and why I believe it is possible to "agree to disagree" without viewing one another with harsh judgment or incorrect assumptions. As Saint Augustine said, "In essentials, unity; in non-essentials, liberty; in all things, charity."[4]

The doctrine of the Trinity was formalized at the Council of Nicaea in AD 325, concluding that Jesus was "one in being or substance" with the Father.[5] At the Council of Constantinople in AD 381, the Father and Son were reaffirmed as being "one," and the divinity of the Holy Spirit was affirmed.[6] Since then, the theology of the Trinity has been reaffirmed and expanded upon by many theologians but has remained true to its fundamentals: that God is three unique persons who operate as one.

From this unified foundation, however, two different viewpoints have emerged on how the members of the Godhead relate to and interact with one another. According to Kevin Giles, in his book *The Trinity & Subordinationism*, this theological debate has been written about more in the last thirty years than any other Christian doctrine.[7] It is one that theologians continue to wrestle with year after year.

Both sides agree that all members of the Trinity are equal in value and importance, and that their relationship to one another is based on mutual love and respect. One view, however, holds that the Trinity is a picture of three equal persons bound together in unity and mutually submitting to and indwelling one another. It is a wholly integrated relationship. When Jesus came to earth, He temporarily gave up this equal status with the Father and Holy Spirit in order to enter fully into humanity. He voluntarily became subordinate to the Father, but His equality was reestablished after He was raised from the dead and ascended into heaven. This is called an "egalitarian view" and is based on the French word *égale*, meaning "equal."[8]

The second view holds Jesus' role as subordinate to the Father while on earth was not temporary but is how His relationship with the Father is continuously. Although all three persons of the Trinity are equal in value, there is a hierarchy in their roles and how they function with one another. Just as the Father commanded and Jesus obeyed Him while on earth, this has always been their positional relationship, and always will be. The Father lovingly cares for and directs Jesus according to His will, and Jesus obeys. Jesus joyfully and willingly submits to the Father, and the Holy Spirit does the same to Jesus. This is a "hierarchical view," and the theology of Jesus being in an eternal role "under" the Father continuously is called "eternal subordination."[9]

Egalitarian View of the Trinity	Hierarchical View of the Trinity
Father / Holy Spirit / Son (circular arrows)	Father → Son → Holy Spirit (downward arrows)

Both sides believe that all three divine persons of the Trinity are of equal value, display love and unity, and are clearly demonstrated throughout Scripture. Both sides also agree that the doctrine of the Trinity should inform how people, who are made in God's image, should relate and interact with one another. As you can see, this belief in who God is greatly changes our understanding of who we are as people and how He wants us to live and lead in our homes, churches, workplaces, and communities.

People who hold an egalitarian view of the Trinity often believe that men and women are equal in being and are free to fulfill any role in the home, in church, at work, or in community based on their individual giftedness and calling as validated by the community. Men and women, though different, are equal and complement one another without hierarchy. Relationships between men and women are built upon mutuality; the goal is mutual servanthood, mutual submission, and mutual respect. Their relationships are a true partnership, where either one is incomplete without the other. They tend to downplay a division between sacred and secular, so this mutuality is lived out in all roles and all environments—such as home, church, work—alike. Egalitarians hold to the inerrancy of Scripture and believe that their position is God's reconciling work to restore human relationships to reflect the egalitarian relationships of the Trinity.

People who follow the hierarchical view of the Trinity believe that men and women are equal in value but have different roles and functions because of the gender God has given them, including roles of leading and roles of following. Relationships between men and women have an established and God-ordained order that, if lived out in Christlikeness, creates freedom and peace for everyone. Women are uniquely created to be "helpmates" to men, and their gifts and perspectives complement and often play a large role in the success of a man's leadership, work, and ministry. Because of the "helpmate" and "complement" roles of women, this perspective is often known as the "complementarian" viewpoint.

Complementarians tend to emphasize the centrality of marriage as the cornerstone of the family, church, community, and, therefore, all of society. Wives will often "come alongside" their husbands to assist them in their various roles and responsibilities, including family, church leadership, and even their secular work. Complementarians hold to the inerrancy of Scripture and believe that their position is God's reconciling work to restore human relationships to reflect the hierarchical relationships of the Trinity.

There are some widespread misconceptions and fears about both sides; however, I have found that both viewpoints speak out strongly against abuse or oppression of any kind. Both hold to God's establishment of two clear genders, male and female, and the value and importance of each, including the traditional marriage relationship. Neither theology approves of homosexuality, transgenderism, or gender neutrality. In addition, neither position takes their viewpoint to the extreme of one gender being more important or "better" than the other gender, such as extreme patriarchy/misogyny or matriarchy/extreme feminism.

Although there are two primary theological viewpoints, egalitarianism and complementarianism, in my experience and in the perspectives of the women interviewed and surveyed for this project, these two viewpoints get lived out in *a lot* of different ways. Even within denominations that have very clear and published theological positions, individual local congregations will many times draw different "lines" for what a woman can do in their church in either direction. In addition, with the rise of nondenominational churches, there is even more opportunity for various expressions. The issue can get further complicated if a female leader has been involved in more than one church, and especially if she has been in different parts of the country where the culture of the community often influences how gender is lived out in various ministry roles.

Following is an outline of what I have found to be the most common cultural practices regarding women in leadership.[10] Again, this is simply meant to be a helpful tool for you to have a starting place for bringing clarity to your church and leaders. Your culture may not fit squarely into one category. Use this as an opportunity to explore the mixed messages you might be sending the female leaders in your church and how you might be able to bring clarity that results in greater leadership capacity for them and your ministry. In addition, I should mention that this simple outline, also available in chart form on my website,[11] cannot fully represent or adequately articulate each viewpoint or the many ways they are lived out, but hopefully I have represented everyone equally.

Extreme Feminism/Matriarchal

- *Biblical viewpoint:* Scriptures are often distorted, ignored, or used out of context.
- *Basic beliefs about gender roles:* Women are superior to men, they are smarter and more caring, and, therefore, they should hold higher levels of leadership in home, church, work, and communities/politics.
- *At home:* Women are strong (even aggressive) in their leadership at home; husbands tend to be passive.
- *At church:* Although there aren't many available examples of this, it is assumed women at church would run similar to women at home.
- *At work or in the local community:* Women are more capable than men to lead at work or in communities. There is a strong sense of women fighting to hold more and higher levels of leadership than men.

Strong Egalitarian (also called Evangelical Feminism)

- *Biblical viewpoint:* Scriptures are egalitarian, with a sense of advocating for women's rights or places of leadership because of past male domination.
- *Basic beliefs about gender roles:* Men and women are fully equal in value and leadership opportunities based on individual gifting and calling.
- *At home:* Men and women are equals, with an emphasis on mutual submission and partnership. Roles are collaboratively decided based on giftedness and preference. It would be common for either a man or a woman to stay home with small children or for both to work.
- *At church:* Men and women are equal and able to fulfill all roles

of leadership based on the community's validation of one's giftedness and calling. Women are embraced in leadership, including being a senior leader of a congregation.

- *At work or in the local community:* Men and women are completely equal in the workplace.

Mild Egalitarian

- *Biblical viewpoint:* Scriptures are egalitarian.
- *Basic beliefs about gender roles:* Men and women are equal partners in home, church, and work.
- *At home:* Roles are based on personal giftedness and preference. There is a high sense of teamwork and supporting each other equally in home life, parenting, and career opportunities. There is shared decision making, with an emphasis on compromise. It would be common for a man to make dinner every night because he enjoys cooking, and a woman to pay the bills because she is good with finances.
- *At church:* All roles and leadership positions are open for men and women equally. However, in practice, many churches have more men in leadership roles than women. Women lead on their own merits and are not required to be married to a pastor to have high levels of influence and authority, including teaching/preaching.
- *At work or in the local community:* Men and women are completely equal in the workplace.

Complementarian/Egalitarian Crossover

- *Biblical viewpoint:* Scriptures combine egalitarian and complementarian viewpoints and practices.
- *Basic beliefs about gender roles:* Men and women are equal and

have individual giftings that tend to be connected to gender, but there is space for differences. A preference for final male leadership or authority is common.

- *At home:* Roles are similar and are usually based on giftedness and preference. There is a high sense of teamwork, but most women choose to prioritize children over career, while most men choose to be the breadwinner. Decisions are made together, but the husband would break a tie if needed (which is rare). There is a sense of husbands and wives completing each other and of mutual submission.

- *At church:* Most roles can be filled by either a man or a woman based on giftedness and effectiveness, although the highest level of leadership positions (senior pastors and/or elders) are reserved for or preferred to be men. Women may preach but usually with a male "covering." Women may lead in some high-level organizational leadership roles or because they are married to men in higher pastoral leadership. Although the majority of leaders will be men, some women may hold the title "pastor" or there may be gender-neutral titles for everyone (i.e., ministry director).

- *At work or in the local community:* Men and women are equal in the workplace and are encouraged to pursue career success. However, women are encouraged and celebrated when they stay home with young children and value family over career.

Mild Complementarian

- *Biblical viewpoint:* Scriptures are hierarchical for home and church where there is "spiritual authority."
- *Basic beliefs about gender roles:* Men and women are equal in value but have different primary roles; there is more freedom in secondary roles. Home and church operate differently than work.
- *At home:* Some roles are clearly different, while some may

be based on ability or preference. Women are homemakers and the primary caregivers to children; men are the primary breadwinners and leaders of the family. The husband is considered the leader and has the final decision-making rights but will often involve his wife in the decision-making process.

- *At church:* Formal and high-level leadership roles are reserved for men, but women may have several formal or informal leadership roles that do not involve having "spiritual authority" over men. Women freely lead other women or children under eighteen and on occasion, women may be included in team teaching or as guest speakers with "covering" or approval by the male senior pastor/elders. Pastors' wives tend to be more involved in leadership alongside or as extensions of their husbands' authority. There is often a strong women's ministry where women have freedom to lead.

- *At work or in the local community:* There is a clear distinction between roles at home and church and opportunities at work. Women are free and often pursue lifelong careers, including leadership roles, although most choose to stay home with small children.

Strong Complementarian

- *Biblical viewpoint:* Scriptures are hierachical.
- *Basic beliefs about gender roles:* Men and women are equal in value but different in their roles. The man is considered the "head" and the woman the "helpmate."
- *At home:* A man's primary role is to provide servant leadership and be the breadwinner for his wife and children. A woman's primary role is to be submissive to her husband's leadership and manage the home and children until they are adults. Decisions are solely made by the husband.

- *At church:* Men hold all roles of leadership and authority, including elders, pastors, preachers, deacons, and team leaders; the only exception would be women's ministries but even those would be under the direction of a male pastoral leader. Women may fill service roles in the church but only those that would not involve any form of leadership over men. Women are not allowed to teach in ministry settings or seminaries.
- *At work or in the local community:* A woman's primary focus is being a homemaker and raising children. Although some may work outside the home as long as their family responsibilities are not compromised, roles of authority (such as a police officer or holding political office) are not appropriate.

Patriarchal

- *Biblical viewpoint:* Scriptures are often distorted, ignored, or used out of context.
- *Basic beliefs about gender roles:* Men are superior to women and should lead in all areas of life. There are biological, psychological, and intellectual differences between genders that make each suitable for their role.
- *At home:* Roles are based on gender, with men in leadership roles and women in submissive roles in all aspects of home life. Women often wear skirts, no makeup, and let their hair grow; there is often tight control of how they spend their time.
- *At church:* Men hold all positions of leadership and authority. Ministries and activities are often separated between adult men and women and children. If a woman needs help at home (for example, her husband is abusing her), she is to come to the church leadership for resolution rather than the authorities, such as the police or a women's shelter.
- *At work or in the local community:* A woman should not work if

she is married, and especially if she has children. Some may even question her need for an education.

Spend some time with your team and other leaders talking through your own theological understanding and your church's beliefs. Compare this to your everyday common practices. Do they line up? Where are the discrepancies? Would someone in your congregation be able to see the alignment, or is there likely confusion? How well are your congregation and volunteer leaders living out these beliefs?

Although this may open up some uncomfortable dialogue, the female leaders in your church need you to bring clarity and consistency to these issues. If you are like most churches, 61 percent of your congregation is female[12] and they are likely holding back. You have the opportunity to give them the clarity they need to lead fully and confidently, for the benefit of your entire church.

Best Practice #3

3

MINE THE MARKETPLACE

I loved the small church I grew up in. It was filled with authentic believers who knew God's Word, loved people in very practical ways, and spent most of their spare time and energy volunteering, especially to help single moms, kids, and youth. Even our founding pastor was bi-vocational and owned a successful electric company to support his family. It wasn't until I went to college that I learned some people are actually *paid* to work in ministry and that there were such things as denominations. I just thought that when you got saved, your whole life went to Jesus and serving in ministry, with no expectation of getting anything back. (Wouldn't it be great if every believer in our churches lived like this?)

Because I had given my life to the Lord and wanted to serve Him in the best way possible, I planned to do what I thought every godly woman does . . . marry a pastor and run the children's program, along with having at least four kids. No one ever told me I should do this, nor did I ever have a conversation with anyone about it. I'm not even sure I gave it any actual critical thought. It was just what I had observed, and somehow I had absorbed those assumptions throughout my childhood and young adult years. And because I thought I could do both well, I ended up an education major and engaged to a pastoral student.

But something wasn't right. I was just learning how to really listen to the Holy Spirit and discern God's specific direction for my life. Long story short, I ended up breaking up with the future pastor and decided to fully surrender all hopes of being married or a mother and instead became a nurse with plans to head overseas to be a medical missionary. Apparently that was the other option I thought was available: lifelong singleness and living in a third-world country, wearing skirts every day, and delivering babies. Thankfully, God is not deterred by our assumptions or cultural norms.

Now, I'll admit, a little piece of me longs to make a frontline difference the way I think a missionary does (maybe I will start that orphanage one day), but the journey God has taken me on is so incredibly different, and so much more equipping for the ministry leadership roles I've had, that I can't deny He had a plan for me I simply could not see at the time.

And I'm not alone.

Every one of the high-level female leaders we interviewed and 95 percent of those surveyed have worked in a non-ministry career. They have been given projects to manage, a staff to lead, and initiatives to implement. They have received formal and informal leadership development and have withstood the rigors of the business world. Even women who went to seminary commented on the incredible training and lessons they learned in the marketplace that equipped them for their current ministry leadership.

Here are some of the professional roles women from our survey have had, and they are now using those skills for the kingdom:

attorney
district sales manager
hotel vice president
COO/CEO
executive director/president
oil industry executive
realtor
banker
government/nonprofit executive
doctor/dentist
pharmacy salesperson
human resources director
staffing manager
retail store manager
small business owner/entrepreneur
marketing executive
communications director
professional artist/musician
photographer
corporate trainer
engineer (all types)
agro sciences executive
hospitality manager
professional fund-raiser
board of directors chairwoman
athletic director
construction manager
graphics and web designer
publisher/editor/author

principal/teacher
nurse practitioner/manager
sheriff's office manager
university professor/dean
energy consultant
insurance broker
IT/technology executive
licensed counselor/psychotherapist
CPA/finance officer
military officer (all branches)
social worker
business coach
electrician/facilities manager
translator/interpreter
television/media/film
physical/occupational therapist
corporate event planner
account executive

Wouldn't it be wonderful to unleash some of this proven potential in your ministry?

In many cases, these women have had a desire, and even a clear sense of calling, to serve the Lord in ministry. But most have had a difficult time finding a place in their churches to use their gifts and abilities, especially if they were interested in working full-time in ministry. Or perhaps some were like me, and headed into a non-church career with the assumption that being a volunteer worker in church was the most that would ever be available to them.

Either way, when I talk to women leaders, many of them still have a strong desire to work or lead in ministry. Never assume that an established, professional female leader isn't interested in working with or for you. Many incredible leaders would love the opportunity to use their marketplace skills in the kingdom. I know several women who have given up very high-profile and well-paid professional careers to serve in ministry, and their impact has been amazing.

Before becoming a church multisite director, Kathy was an executive vice president at the fifth-largest bank in the country. She led eleven thousand retail employees across twenty-five hundred locations and was listed as one of the Top 25 Women in Banking before life took a turn and God opened up a role for her at her church.

She said, "At the bank I was focused on mobilizing my team and developing our youngest bankers. I got a chance to grow a lot of people and help them develop. I learned how to coach, which has been very helpful. So now I only have fourteen campus locations, and I don't have to get on a plane every day. And the campus pastors don't lie to me. In comparison, this church job is pretty easy!"[1]

THE CHALLENGES OF DEVELOPING FEMALE LEADERS

I've been working in the leadership development space for more than twenty-five years, and like most people, I am a huge proponent of growing leaders "from within," especially in local church contexts. This is challenging work, but it is even harder when it comes to growing female leaders.

In the business world, it is well documented that women have a difficult time advancing in leadership. They often receive less training, have fewer resources, and are paid less than their male counterparts. Even though entry-level roles are nearly split between men and women, women are 18 percent less likely to be promoted to a manager, and with each level of leadership, their likelihood of being promoted gets even less, resulting in 81 percent men and only 19 percent women in the C-suite. For women of color, the percentages are even lower.[2]

But it won't always be this way. As women begin to fulfill leadership roles throughout an organization, the internal systems will become more welcoming, have more female leader involvement in trainings, and be accessed by younger female leaders. All of this will eventually turn a culture. Until this kind of significant change happens, however, churches need to take a "both/and" approach to leadership development—develop from within *and* leverage what the marketplace has already invested and tested.

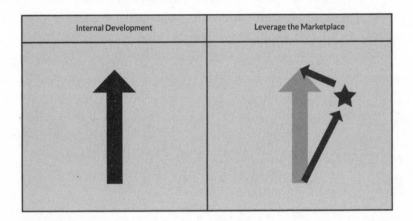

Internal Development	Leverage the Marketplace

One of the advantages the church has is to be able to watch and interact with leaders long before offering them a job. Volunteering is the best job interview process ever. Consider it your farm league system. Look around. Who is spiritually leading well? Who seems to resonate with your culture? Who is succeeding? Who is developing people? Who is naturally building a team? Those are your leaders.

Accessing female leaders who have already proven themselves in other professions *and* in your volunteer roles are gold and are worth going after. There are a few caveats, however. Here are some tips for picking the right women to add to your team.

MAKE SURE YOU HIRE ONLY
GREAT FEMALE LEADERS.

Nothing kills momentum for female leadership more than hiring low-quality, unproven, or ineffective leaders. This issue was mentioned several times in our conversations with female leaders, and many had experienced being held back in their own leadership advancement due to a low-performing female leader who went ahead of them. This is an unfortunate consequence of being in a minority. If a man performs poorly in a job, it doesn't affect our view of all men on the team. But the same is not true for women trying to break into male-dominated environments.

There is a difference between women who have the basic skills and gifts to grow and perform well and those who simply *want* to lead. Just because a woman *wants* to lead doesn't mean she is a skilled leader. Be sure to test her in real environments, look for actual fruit, hold a full interview and screening process, and check all background references. Avoid taking on someone who still needs a lot of personal and basic leadership development. That person can go into your development system and grow over time. When you are creating space for women leaders, make sure that space is reserved for those who already display basic leadership competency. You are sifting for gold; don't be fooled by a shiny rock.

GIVE THE FEMALE LEADERS YOU
HIRE *REAL* LEADERSHIP JOBS.

Andrea and her husband met in college and received the same ministry education, although she had more ministry leadership experience from her student years and serving on the mission field. When they graduated, a church hired both of them. He was offered the role of high school student pastor, and she was offered a role as an administrative assistant.

I remember being frustrated in that administrative role because I wanted to be serving in the youth service on Wednesday night, but instead I was known as the one who had the keys and knew how to make the copies. I was so frustrated I finally ended up leaving that position to take a full-time job downtown at a publishing firm so I could be freed up in ministry to just show up and minister to students. That's where my heart was.

Then I was given a similar role at our second church. They hired us together, knowing our skills and gifting, but while my husband was put on pastoral staff, I was asked to be the executive assistant to the senior pastor. The pastor saw more in me and let me help in whatever ministry I wanted, such as leading a Bible study or mentoring staff women, but I still had to do all that on top of this other, non-ministry job. I ended up quitting that job as well and getting another role in construction for the same reasons. It wasn't until I was twenty-nine, had a master's degree, and had two babies that I got my first pastoral role on a church staff as the missions pastor.[3]

Female leaders, especially those you are recruiting from the marketplace, need "real jobs" with real titles. Administrative assistants are incredibly valuable on any team (I could not survive without mine), but their gifting and contribution are very different from those of a leader. Administrative skills are not the same as the spiritual gift of administration.

Administrative skills include organizing, scheduling, computing, detail management, planning, and so forth. These are often skills that are helpful in supporting a person or events and are usually performed behind the scenes. The *gift of administration*, on the other hand, is based on the Greek word *kybernesis*, a unique term referring to a shipmaster or captain. It literally means "to steer" or "to rule or govern," and implies guiding or directing a group of people toward a goal.[4] This gift is similar to a gift of leadership, but is usually more oriented to organization, structure, and accomplishing tasks to achieve the goal.

As you can probably guess, putting someone with the gift of leadership or administration into an administrative assistant role will be frustrating for her and unproductive in the long term for you. Resist the urge to "get someone on the team" or help her "learn the culture" from an assistant role. This goes for leaders in your pipeline as well. Create a new or unique role instead. It would be better to hire a talented leader at quarter time or on a contract basis in a significant leadership role than to hire her full-time in a job designed to be primarily supportive, behind-the-scenes, or administrative in nature. The only exception would be if you start out all high-level leaders, including middle-aged professional white men, in administrative assistant roles. I actually know one church that does that!

PAY FEMALE LEADERS FAIRLY.

Most marketplace leaders who transition into ministry knowingly give up salary, benefits, and all sorts of perks. The least we can do is pay them fairly for their years of experience, leadership ability, and unique expertise. The salary package you offer female leaders needs to be equivalent to men doing the same type and level of work. Even if you choose to give them a different title (director instead of pastor), be sure to fairly evaluate if their span of leadership, level of responsibility, and number of hours worked each week is significantly lower to necessitate a difference in pay. Simply being "on call" for the pastoral emergency phone number a couple of times a year or performing weddings, for which most pastors receive additional pay, is usually not enough to warrant a different pay scale. If you have expectations that she will spiritually care for those under her leadership, for example, women or families, she deserves the same pay a pastor receives.

It is also discriminatory to pay a woman less because she is not the "breadwinner" of her home or based solely on her gender. I know one female executive pastor who donates her entire paycheck back to the church because her family does not need it. How different her employment and the value she experiences from her leaders would have been had she been recruited to work for low pay because her family didn't need the money.

I was recruited into my first ministry role after serving as a dean at a university. I had no idea that pastors received tax benefits or different insurance options than the rest of the staff. It wasn't until more than a year into my job when I made my first staff hire—a man who would work for me overseeing weekend and event teams—that I discovered he would be getting a ministry tax benefit and paid insurance for his whole family. I was blessed to work for very godly leaders who, once I brought the issue to their attention, had no idea about my benefits discrepancy and fixed it immediately.

Apparently, when the human resource team had processed my employment paperwork, they automatically put me in the "clerical" category since they had never hired a woman into a leadership role before. And because I was new to ministry, the only thing I knew to negotiate when hired was my annual salary and time off. In their defense, I did have a confusing "girl title" and didn't exactly fit into any existing category, but these are elements you need to pay particular attention to when you recruit female leaders from the marketplace.

Eventually, any inconsistency will be discovered, and as one of my good ministry friends (a male executive pastor) says, "Just make sure you can pass the 'Red Face Test.' If someone were to discover this information, would your face turn red?" This is always a test worth taking in private before you have to experience it in public.

GIVE FEMALE LEADERS PLATFORM TIME.

Nothing communicates leadership and authority in the church like being on the stage during a worship service. Whether the person is a worship leader, making an announcement about an upcoming event, or preaching the sermon, the individuals on the platform are personally recognized by the congregation and are assumed to have some sort of position or authority in the church. In my opinion, being onstage in church is the equivalent of having the corner office in a business. No one may know what you do or what your title is, but the office says everything they need to know. And that is true of standing on the church stage as well.

Regardless of your stance on a woman teaching the message, if you want her to be able to lead well in your church, she needs to have regular opportunities to be in front during weekend services. I'm an advocate of this for any leader—campus pastor, small group coordinator, children's ministry director, and even the guy who runs the setup/takedown team. A woman is going to have an easier job leading if she is brought up onstage and acknowledged for her service. She doesn't even have to say anything. The pastor can do all the talking, but her recruiting responsibilities just got a lot easier now that every person in the congregation has seen her face, learned what she leads, and watched the pastor appreciate her and her contribution. The next time she walks into the student center and needs to move the chairs around, all the volunteers will jump up to help her because they now know she has the authority to lead.

Jenni Catron, a leadership consultant and a former church executive director, works with church leaders and has a unique view of some of the widespread systemic issues that hold women back from leading effectively:

> The most glaring thing I see is that women lack early opportunities to be up front. And I do not mean just teaching on Sunday

mornings. I mean leading meetings, doing announcements, or being onstage to develop her presentation or teaching gifts.

The unexpected gift of my corporate experience was I was part of the sales and marketing team. At twenty years old I learned how to give a sales presentation to a room of fifty-year-old sales guys. That skill of presenting and speaking in front of people obviously became a huge gift inside the church because we know leaders need that skill to be able to lead a team and meetings well.

In many churches, women aren't given the opportunity to be up front because they lack the experience to do it well. I have seen this to be especially true in some of our larger churches. When I ask the pastors about it, I often hear, "I would really love to put women in those positions, but I don't have any who are at the level that I feel they can teach and hold their own."

And while this may be true, unfortunately this makes the women more insecure and less confident with every lost opportunity. It communicates that their leaders don't believe in them when they pick a guy with more experience instead of them.

Accordingly, the systemic issue I see is that women aren't given enough opportunities to learn those skills, which means they can't use those skills. Therefore, men dominate our platforms. I'm not championing that women need to be preaching every Sunday, but I think when women are on the platform, it really makes a big difference—sometimes in ways we don't even realize.

In fact, last week I talked with a woman who serves in an executive pastor role where her senior leaders have been intentional about having her do different things from the stage, like giving the announcements. She said every time she does it, somebody comes up to her and tells her the weight her presence holds. One woman shared, "I love that you are up front because my daughter brought another eighth-grade girl to youth group who saw you onstage along with a female worship leader. The girl went home and told her mom that she wanted to go back to church because she wanted to do what you ladies do. Now their whole family has started attending our church because that young girl saw women onstage and felt like they were role models for her."[5]

We don't realize the unintentional consequences of not making women visible in our churches. They lack that visibility because they lack the opportunities, and they lack the opportunities because they have not developed the necessary skills. It's a self-fulfilling cycle that needs to change.

HELP FEMALE LEADERS TRANSITION INTO MINISTRY.

When we "grow up" in a profession of any kind, there are certain customs, rituals, and filters that we naturally learn and therefore see the world through. For example, my first profession was nursing. An RN's goal is to help patients get better. We assess the patient, treat the patient, and measure how the patient is progressing. Every action we take is based on the *individual* patient and his or her *individual* progress. Likewise, as I work in ministry, one of the first things I look for is how our programs and systems affect *individuals* and each person's *individual* faith journey.

But I've worked with people who grew up professionally in other industries and initially look for different measures of success. For example, sales and marketing people are not necessarily as concerned with the individual. Significant sales are made when a significant number of people are impacted, so they are looking for changes that will impact *lots* of people. Their natural orientation is to focus on getting a lot of people to grow a little, while my natural orientation is to get a few people to grow a lot. Both are right and helpful, but they are very different approaches.

Your ministry also has priorities and perspectives that are likely different from what a professional in another industry has learned.

Simply being in a church and volunteering in ministry is not the same as understanding your staff's culture and the priorities, practices, and expectations of ministry leadership. It is important to teach these filters and assumptions to anyone coming into leadership from the marketplace.

There is also a difference when you are dealing with spiritual matters. Mallory, a former marketplace executive turned executive pastor, described it: "In the corporate world, the goal is to go higher. Higher-level decisions. Higher responsibility. Higher influence. But in ministry, every step is weightier. It's hard to learn how to separate the weight from your own soul. The stress is different. You just don't know what it's doing to you. I've had to learn it's not the sprint; it's the 'steady' that matters."[6]

Soul care, spiritual warfare, balancing weekend and evening hours, changes in friendships within the congregation, confidentiality, expectations on her family, increased attention to her looks and clothing (yes, it's a thing), less direct contact with unbelievers, and questioning, *How do I know if I'm doing a good job?* are all issues and challenges that affected and usually surprised the women leaders we interviewed. Tara Beth commented, "I serve at an incredibly affirming church, but my looks are a constant topic of conversation. Not a Sunday passes when someone doesn't comment on my hair or my outfit."[7]

If your culture has a six-day workweek, this can also be a big transition. Although most high-level leaders work more than a forty-hour workweek these days, the need to be at church six days a week, at all the services, with limited time off, and with varying levels of flexibility, left many women leaders on a quick road to burnout. "There's just no downtime," one female leader said. "With services every weekend and something happening all through the summer plus every holiday, it's hard to catch your breath. At least in the business world there were 'on' and 'off' seasons."[8]

Women tend to be less stringent about boundaries than men, especially if they are new to a job, so they can fall into the trap of doing more than is being asked of them. It is critical to clarify your expectations, help them know what a "win" looks like for them, and free them from feeling obligated to attend every single thing that happens at the church.

The biggest challenge, however, tends to be navigating the minefield of various levels of approval and support from male leaders within the staff. According to a Barna Study about women leaders in the church, "Most women say they are fully supported in pursuing leadership roles by the men in their lives, including their senior pastors and their husbands." However, 54 percent of female leaders do not feel supported by *other* male leaders in their church.[9] This can create a lot of tension on teams when a woman is trying to lead initiatives that affect more than just her department. This "friendly fire" was especially common for women who were the only female on the leadership team.

In addition, you may need to coach her on leading well when someone on her team is disappointed he now has a female leader. As you continue to add female leaders to the team, these issues will become fewer and fewer. As one woman executive pastor put it, "Once there was a second woman on our leadership team, everything got better."[10] Having more than one female often helps neutralize the gender issues and also gives a sense of support and assistance when there is conflict over gender biases.

Any professional who transitions into ministry will need guidance, and women are no exception. But since there are fewer role models and more difficult dynamics, you'll have to be more intentional to bring up these conversations, offer coaching, and provide resources to help a female leader transition in a way that keeps her healthy and fruitful in the marathon of ministry.

SUPPORT FEMALE LEADERS' HUSBANDS AND FAMILIES.

Supporting pastors' and ministers' wives is a consistent topic of conversation in ministry settings. It's not uncommon to have several offerings for wives at conferences, staff retreats, elder meetings, or even within a church's monthly programming and budgets. By the way, be sure to let your female staff leaders know they should go to the leadership meetings and not the wives' meetings. This can be very confusing at first! But not one of the churches represented by the women we interviewed had developed any unique programs or systems to support ministry husbands.

Ashley, a young female leader new to a student ministry pastoral role, described it like this:

> I think churches who ask a woman to be high up in leadership, especially with the title "pastor," need to think about her family in a different way. They need to be brought along in a healthy way, protected and supported, and given space to be a family together. If my husband were to feel forgotten or unnoticed, I would never be able to do ministry well. It can be especially hard to manage when leaders communicate they care about your family if they've never even reached out or had an authentic conversation with your husband.[11]

A male staff member is often more apt to advocate for his wife if she's feeling disconnected, lonely, or even depressed, but for a female leader it's a double-edged sword. She doesn't want to make her husband look needy or too vulnerable, and yet he can feel out of place when his wife is well connected at the church and he is sitting in the service alone while she's working.

One female executive pastor was excited when an elder called her husband and asked him to lunch. Unfortunately, instead of building a relationship with him, the elder spent the entire meal interrogating him about their marriage and home life. That was not exactly the support her husband or she was hoping for.

At Life.Church, one of the largest churches in America, however, they have taken a slightly different approach. Rather than singling out pastors' wives, they simply have small groups, special events, and gatherings for "staff spouses" and "staff families." Jerry Hurley, the executive pastor of team development, explained how they do it:

> We work hard to integrate spouses into our organization. What I tell our team is that, as a general rule of thumb, you have to realize that we are in a spiritual battle. Our spouses are just close enough to the battle to be wounded, so we need to make sure that they're close enough to all the great things about this ministry to stay connected and excited about it. If all a spouse ever hears is the complaint or the negative stuff, that is not going to serve them well.
>
> We work really hard to keep all spouses, regardless of gender, connected. We have Facebook groups. We invite spouses to our staff meetings and stream them online for spouses who work (male and female) or can't attend. If we have a staff training around Myers-Briggs or Emotional Intelligence, we invite spouses so they can learn these things alongside their spouse. If a staff member, their spouse, or a child needs counseling, we pay for that. Once a year we have a "Family Reunion" where all staff and spouses come together from all our campuses for three days. It's a wonderful time together. It's really our mind-set and intention to keep everyone connected and cared for.[12]

Working to keep ministry husbands connected doesn't mean you need to go out of your way to roll out programs and force connections with them. In fact, many of the female leaders we talked to were thankful their husbands weren't required to be out extra nights for spousal obligations. The biggest thing you can do is simply take the time and effort, as a leader in your church, to authentically connect and care about the families under your spiritual care. Few other people in the church will do this for someone in a leadership role, and even fewer will think to do it for a female leader. Building relationships and pastoring the families of your female leaders will not only help them thrive at your church, but it also will free them to lead fully.

AND FINALLY, DON'T SET FEMALE LEADERS UP ON A "GLASS CLIFF."

In addition to the "glass ceiling," new research has emerged about the "glass cliff." In the early to mid-2000s, a series of media reports implied that having women on the board or as CEO negatively impacted the company's performance. When this was researched further, the conclusion was that the media had gotten it wrong: the opposite was true, and a new phenomenon was revealed. The poor-performing companies that had women as CEOs were actually in decline when they hired the women, and most of the time, under those women's leadership, the companies turned around. Even more interesting, once a company started performing well again, most of those female CEOs were replaced by men. The "glass cliff," then, is a metaphor describing these high-risk opportunities that are often given to women.[13]

This "glass cliff" effect showed up in many of the interviews of high-level female leaders. Although none of them used these words or had even thought of it in this way, many had experiences where they were given opportunities to lead that had quite different circumstances than the men on their team had—a "turn around" or crisis scenario with higher risk, a higher chance of failure, with extra work and effort required—and they often underwent higher levels of criticism than a more typical leadership assignment. Most of the women had interpreted these opportunities as positive—that her leaders believed in her and her abilities, perhaps even more than those of the men, to have given her such a troubled situation—and they were proud to have risen to the occasion.

The challenge is that this often sets up women for a higher risk of failure and the need to endure higher levels of stress and criticism. Burnout in these types of roles tends to be higher as well, since most women are not compensated for the extra time, effort, and work. Although there are several theories about why this happens, the most accepted is that because opportunities to lead for women are rarer, they are more willing to take a risk and make personal sacrifices for the chance to lead. Churches that may be having trouble getting a leader to successfully take on such a risky area are usually willing to let a female leader give it a try if she is willing. Male leaders, on the other hand, have options to stay or get another job rather than find themselves, and their career, on the edge of a risky cliff.

As you bring females onto your staff in leadership roles, be sure to set them up to succeed. Educate yourself on the natural bias and tendencies that create either glass ceilings or glass cliffs. Talk about this concept openly, and work as a team to take on challenging, high-risk roles so that everyone wins (or loses) together.

Mining the marketplace to find high-level female leaders not only builds up your gender diversity, but it also affords you important expertise and skill sets for which your team wouldn't normally have access. Many of the unique contributions I have been able to make in my various ministry roles have been from education and experiences outside the church but have greatly benefited our ministries. This includes everything from producing musical-theater performances, to understanding mental health assessments, to developing human resource policies and building leadership training programs. There's no telling the kinds of rich backgrounds and professional acumen the women in your congregations have to offer your staff team and your church.

There's a reason Jesus instructs us to pray for workers for the harvest. We all need great leaders who will show up and can be trusted to lead well. When they succeed, it won't be because of us. It will be because God has been hand-crafting their journey for this very moment. May we all strike gold.

4

INTEGRATE SPIRITUAL FORMATION AND LEADERSHIP DEVELOPMENT

You cannot lead people where you have never been. You cannot impart what you do not possess. You cannot preach with power what you are not practicing with integrity.

—ROD ROGERS, *PASTOR DRIVEN STEWARDSHIP*[1]

I ntegration is a powerful word. It denotes harmony, teamwork, alignment, unity, and synergy. Jesus loved to teach in an integrated way, especially with His disciples. Living together, traveling together, learning together, ministering together, debriefing together, laughing together, leading together, and struggling together were all ways that Jesus raised up spiritually strong leaders capable of moving His mission forward.

The opposite of integration is separation. It denotes disconnection, gaps, discord, segregation, splits, silos, misalignment, and divorce. Unfortunately, for most women, their education and development have been more of a "separation" than an "integration." This is especially true for female leaders in the church.

One of the women I interviewed remembers being halfway through Bible school when she showed up to her first day of Expository Preaching class, excited to combine her love for God's Word with her success on the speech team. She sat in the front row and was promptly asked by the professor, "How did you get in here? This is a male-only class. You can only take Message Prep for Women."[2] And this was fewer than twenty-five years ago.

I grew into a young adult during the Promise Keepers and Women of Faith era. It was a powerful time in the American Christian church, as men and women were hungry to recommit their lives to Christ, and symbolic walls between church communities were being broken down. For me, however, it was always a little confusing. I was leading as a high-level volunteer and heard all these guys I served with come back and tell stories of being inspired to rise up, rallying at the altar with thousands of other men around the call on their lives to make a difference, learning how to lead with character and integrity, and staying up late into the night with their spiritual brothers, praying, confessing sin, and surrendering their whole lives to the Lord. It sounded amazing.

When I attended my first Women of Faith conference, it was great, but it was very different from what the men had described. We had pajama parties at night, with lots of chocolate. Our hotel conversations were about skincare. I heard multiple teachings on how it's (apparently) hard for me to make good decisions because I'm overwhelmed with confusing emotions and deep insecurity. I walked away with a reminder that I am loved and have value, as well as several candles, a homemade picture frame, and a jar of nice-smelling lotion. The disciple in me appreciated the message and loved the two days away to focus on my walk with Christ, but the leader in me longed for something much more.

The subject of women-only discipleship (aka women's ministry) came up in nearly every interview. It was always acknowledged that, for many women, these environments are exactly what they need and can be very effective. But for these strong female leaders, they usually felt quite out of place, like misfits. They could appreciate it, but it didn't speak to the challenges and character issues they personally were facing. Their wiring and giftedness had implications on their spiritual development that these environments were not only leaving unaddressed but were frequently creating an additional tension as they tried to navigate the question: Who am I as a Christ-following woman if I am gifted to lead? As Andrea, an executive pastor, stated, "Leading and Christ-following are interconnected."[3]

Although we didn't ask this specific question on the survey, many of the respondents commented on this tension in the comment box. Here are some of the ways I have heard it described:

- "I'm just not a girly-girl."
- "My issue is with pride more than insecurity. I'm trying to keep my mouth shut more than trying to learn to 'speak up.'"
- "My rough edges were definitely not welcome there. It wasn't until I met a strong female leader who knew how to channel my energy and perspective that I started to find my way."
- "I was totally out of my element. I tried to be like all the other women, but my struggles were so different. When I talked about the stress of having to fire someone or the challenges of working while raising my kids, I was either met with glazed-over eyes or judgment—neither of which was helpful."
- "Most of the time I just felt like I didn't fit. I didn't dress right.

I didn't care about the right things. I was struggling with the wrong things."

- "I really wanted to learn how to use my gifts to serve the Lord. When I would volunteer, I kept getting assigned to bring a shared dish."
- "I'm more comfortable talking with men about leading than I am talking with women about the latest 'whatever' on social media."
- "I often worry that I'm too much for these other women. I'm not sure if it's intimidation, because I certainly don't feel intimidating. I just know that I can't be fully who I am."[4]

Many of these high-level female leaders eventually had to find other places to grow spiritually, often outside their church, and then figure out how to integrate the things they learned into how they led at work or in ministry. This was often done on her own, or perhaps with a few, usually geographically distant, friends who "got it" and could connect with what God was teaching her and asking of her. It is a very isolated way to grow as a leader and as a follower of Jesus, yet most felt they didn't have any other option.

This integration of spiritual growth and leadership development happens much more naturally for male leaders. It's one of the benefits of being in the "majority." The very culture supports relationship-based spiritual and leadership development of men, especially for those interested in pursuing career ministry.

The challenge is that coming from a perspective where women don't lead, women's ministries are often missing the basic components of leadership development, even within their volunteer structures. Women are usually placed in leadership roles because they are married to a pastor, have the most time to volunteer, or "need to feel a part of things," rather than based on their gifts or abilities.

In addition, it has been my experience that the male pastors who oversee women's ministries spend very little time or energy actually leading and holding these teams accountable for results. It's not that these male pastors don't care, but they are extremely hesitant to get involved. One pastor I used to work with described it to me as a "land mine" because most women on the leadership team were married to his bosses. He did his best to give them what they asked for and did not confront any issues because it simply wasn't worth it.

One time, while on staff at a church, we were invited to a national workshop on figuring out where the future of women's ministry would be heading. I attended along with the female leader of our women's ministry, who was also the senior pastor's wife, and the male pastor who oversaw all our adult discipleship classes and groups. Of the forty-five people in the room, he was the only male. I couldn't believe it. Women make up 61 percent of Protestant congregations,[5] and no other men at those churches felt responsible for where these women's primary discipleship ministry was headed in the future? What a missed opportunity, and it points to the lack of attention many of these women's ministries have received from their male church leaders—who, by the way, control the church's financial resources and the ability to train leaders.

Jill, a leadership coach and retired executive pastor, emphasized the need for churches to invest resources in the spiritual development of female leaders:

> When men are successful in business and have a strong spiritual foundation, they easily thrive in ministry. Many women have not had opportunities to lead, so they start out at a different level. Even with a spiritual gift of leadership, it takes more time to move into a leadership position. Both a strong spiritual foundation *and* a strong leadership foundation is vital to lead well in ministry. I know of many churches who put people into ministry leadership way before they are spiritually ready and it never works out well for anyone.[6]

These gender-based ministries have gone through a lot of adjustments during the last two to three decades, especially with the emergence of mixed-gender small groups as well as many other new ministry programming philosophies. I am not recommending moving in any one direction or another, and there is certainly an important part of discipleship that happens in gender-based relationships (Titus 2:4). But what I am advocating for is the integration of leadership development into your discipleship environments, while paying special attention to those that are women-only or mixed gender to make sure they are getting the same resources and accountability you are giving your other ministries.

My most recent role on a church staff involved the development of a leadership training program to equip men and women for volunteer and staff roles throughout our church campuses and within the community. Hands down, the most powerful aspect of the program was the *integration* of spiritual and leadership development. Many of these leaders were stuck in their growth because they had created "compartments" in their lives. In one place they studied Scripture and talked about spiritual things, and in another they studied leadership and worked on leading people. When we helped them pull these two concepts into one pathway for spiritual leadership development, the light bulbs flashed on and the dots started to connect.

In his book *The Making of a Leader,* Dr. J. Robert Clinton states, "God develops a leader over a lifetime. That development is a function of the use of events and people to impress leadership lessons upon a leader (processing), time, and leader response. Processing is central to the theory. All leaders can point to critical incidents in their lives where God taught them something very important."[7]

The female leaders I interviewed for this project offered up many pivotal moments in their leadership and spiritual development journeys when the integration of their faith and giftedness created a unique synergy that catapulted them forward in their walk with the

Lord and their ability to be fruitfully used by Him. Following are the most common themes or topics that would be good to consider integrating intentionally into your spiritual growth and leadership development initiatives.

DEFINING LEADERSHIP

"What is leadership, exactly?" was a common question in the journey of many of our survey participants, especially when they were still in the "emerging" stage of their development. Following are some definitions and perspectives on leadership that I have found helpful in coaching up-and-coming leaders:

- *Leadership is not a title or position.* It is the ability to influence someone for change. Every disciple is called to spiritually lead the lost by sharing his or her faith, leading them to Christ, and teaching them to obey everything Jesus taught (the Great Commission, Matthew 28). The first step of leadership for every Jesus-follower is to disciple another person.
- *Leadership is a spiritual gift that is given directly by God to build up His church.* Spiritual gifts are either believed to be natural gifts seen early in one's life or a result of salvation and the indwelling of the Holy Spirit. Everyone is gifted in different ways, and all the gifts are important for the body to function. In addition to the gift of leadership, church cultures sometimes ascribe leadership attributes to gifts of teaching, administration, shepherding, and apostleship. For the sake of this conversation, all of these spiritual gifts have aspects of leadership that you might be trying to develop and release.
- *Leadership can be a learned skill set.* Even without a specific gifting, leadership skills and abilities can be learned and refined

over time. These leaders are not necessarily naturally gifted as strong leaders, but they have learned the skills and even the art of leadership through growth and development opportunities. In some cases, learned leaders can outshine naturally gifted leaders simply because they have matured their skill set and character over time.

One of the biggest challenges unique to female leaders is feeling "comfortable" in their leadership. Most feel caught in what is known as the "double bind"—as if they are "too much" or "too little" but never quite right.[8] They often wonder or even worry about how to be strong as a leader and still be authentic in their relationships. In fact, there is staggering research from the marketplace that shows the more successful a man is, the more "likeable" he is.[9] But it is the exact opposite for a woman. The higher in an organization a woman leads, the less "likeable" she becomes. This often leaves female leaders with an impossible choice: *Do I want to be liked or respected?* Unfortunately, few women leaders experience being able to have both, at least at the same time. When women are developing as leaders, this can really play into their confidence and ability to realize their full leadership potential. Working through the spiritual implications of not being "liked" as a part of their calling is an important part of their development.

One famous research project presented a Harvard Business School case study about a real-life, successful female entrepreneur and venture capitalist (Heidi Roizen) to test students' perceptions of men and women in the workplace. Half of the students read the test case study about Heidi "as is." But for the other half, the first name was changed to Howard. Everything else stayed the same. Afterward, the students rated both Heidi and Howard as equally competent based on their identical résumés, yet Howard was rated as a more appealing colleague. Heidi was viewed as selfish and not "the type of person you would want to hire or work for," simply because she was a woman.[10]

The experiment demonstrated that when a man is successful, he is liked more by both men and women. But when a woman is successful, both men and women like her less. This can be even more difficult in a church environment, where relationships and female connections are incredibly influential in one's ability to move ministry forward.

As you can imagine, integrating this conversation and these different aspects of a woman's giftedness is an important part of her development, as well as challenging female leaders to grow in their hunger for feedback and self-awareness. Not every limitation on their leadership is due to gender issues or bias, but how can they discern the difference? Helping them figure out the distinction between their own personal leadership liabilities and what might be a more systemic issue is critical in teaching them what a healthy and confident leader looks like and how they can become effective in ministry.

GIFT IDENTIFICATION AND SERVING OPPORTUNITIES

When it came to understanding their giftedness and how that could be a contribution in a ministry setting, there were four distinct experiences that empowered these female leaders.

1. Learning about the concept of different gifts, and especially having the freedom not to have to be good at everything.
2. The identification of their individual gifts; usually being able to name the top two to three and how they work together in combination, as well as their drawbacks.
3. The affirmation or confirmation of those gifts by leaders within their church community. Although preferred, it didn't have to be a formal leader, just someone they considered further along in his or her faith journey.

4. Connecting their gift with a need in the church that resulted in helping people or serving in a fruitful way. Serving in a "bad fit" was often a setback for a woman in clearly understanding and moving toward her calling with confidence.

Many of these leaders had benefited from their church offering some type of spiritual gift assessment and then utilizing that to help connect them into a "good fit" volunteer role. These assessments can be extremely clarifying for women, especially if they have preconceived ideas about what they should or should not be gifted in based on their gender.

Becca, a female executive pastor, recently had a conversation with one of her college ministry students from her church, where women are empowered in many levels of leadership. This young woman explained that she had just taken a spiritual gifts assessment in class and asked, "Is it okay I scored in leadership?"[11] Even with many strong examples around her, she still felt as if there might be a mistake or that *she* was a mistake.

On the flip side, it was also a common experience for these leaders to discover that traditionally "female gifts," such as hospitality, mercy, helps, and shepherding, were often at the bottom of their list. For many, this created another kind of identity crisis:

- "Am I not a good woman?"
- "Can I be godly if I don't like to cook or entertain?"
- "What does this mean for my ability to be a wife or a mom?"
- "Did God make a mistake?"

How they handled these questions, and the way their churches and leaders supported them in redefining their own expectations of themselves, played a significant role in how these women recalibrated their identity in Christ, the call on their lives, and the formation of a vision around how God might want to use them in service to others. Judy, an executive pastor, said, "It was so freeing when I realized that I didn't prefer working with men over women; I just prefer working with *leaders*. That's why connecting with other strong female leaders, although sometimes hard to find, is so life-giving to me."[12]

It is also worth noting that in our survey, more than 60 percent of the women who are leading in ministries today had their leadership either noticed or affirmed before the age of nineteen. Helping young leaders, both male and female, identify their gifts early on only lengthens their ability to integrate those gifts into their spiritual formation, hopefully creating a solid foundation for a lifetime of ministry.

These assessments are a great front door to the idea of knowing your gifts and how to use them in ministry; however, the conversation shouldn't stop there. Development is a lifelong process, and God usually has more in store for us than we can see, so building in ways for ongoing development and new serving opportunities is key. As ambassador and past general superintendent of the Wesleyan Church, Jo Anne Lyon said, "If we rest on our 'gift,' it's easy to overemphasize it and then you won't step into an opportunity because it isn't 'on my sheet of paper.' But if you *do* step into it, you'll find God has actually gifted you beyond what you realized."[13]

IDENTITY IN CHRIST

The female leaders I interviewed described a time in their lives when they experienced a pivotal turning point. It usually was some sort of faith-leadership crisis in which their security in Christ and their ability to be effective with others was significantly challenged or taken away. God used each one of these unique and personally designed sets of circumstances to teach each leader important lessons about her identity in Christ, her call as a leader, and the unconditional love of her heavenly Father.

Many even acknowledged that limitations placed on them because of their gender were actually tools God used to refine their character and draw them closer to Him. "My journey as a female leader in the church has challenged me to purify my motives," said a survey participant. "I had to get past things being fair, my 'rights' being ignored, my need for recognition or credit, and at times, I had to find my own venues for ministry if the local church didn't support me."[14]

Many female leaders discussed the positive role that professional counseling, inner healing, and working through issues from their families of origin has been to their growth and competency as leaders, especially in spiritual settings. Several also talked about how a woman's thought life can be so much more negative and condemning than a man's. "We women tend to be really hard on ourselves and we make up a lot of stories about what's really going on," said Amy, a church consultant and former church executive director. "I think we have a lot of tracks in our minds that constantly carry shame and negativity. Men would probably be astounded at how many negative thoughts a woman has going on in her head on a given day."[15]

Although every journey and lesson was unique, overall there emerged seven "Identity in Christ" categories that may be helpful as you develop the female leaders in your congregation:

1. I have difficulty fully embracing God's unconditional acceptance without feeling the need to maintain a certain level of performance or accomplishment to "earn or keep His love." Most of the women felt the fear of losing God's love or approval.
2. I need people's approval of me or my leadership.

3. I find security through having control over certain things or people.
4. I feel bad about myself because of my past mistakes, my physical appearance, or things done to me.
5. I blame others or use excuses to defend my poor behavior.
6. I find my significance in being needed.
7. I avoid authenticity because of pressure to "represent Christ or my church" with the appearance of perfection or "having it all together."

Another common facet of identity issues for high-achieving women is known as "Imposter's Syndrome," in which highly competent individuals have a difficult time internalizing their accomplishments and instead have a persistent, underlying fear of being "caught" or "exposed" as a fraud.[16] They often feel they do not deserve the success they have achieved and frequently dismiss their achievements as luck, coincidental timing, or as a result of others giving them more credit than they deserve.

This can be an even deeper identity issue for women in church cultures that overemphasize selflessness, defer credit to others, or spiritualize effective leadership. It is critical to the spiritual development of female leaders to help them learn and practice the difference between minimizing themselves or living in fear and having a whole, healthy identity that gives God the glory while celebrating their amazing achievements.

Amber Smart, a member of the YouVersion launch team and the director of Analytics at Life.Church, shared:

I think my biggest challenge is that whenever I do something, I am "all in." I'm going to go full force into it. There was a season, especially as we were launching YouVersion, when it was really crazy and I lost work-life balance. I look back now and feel sad that there are certain years of my kids' life that I don't really remember much. I have had to learn that I do have a weakness of workaholism, and at the core of that is feeling like if I work hard*er* or the hard*est* or "over and above," then the people around me will have to like me, or even love me, because I've proven it to them. I realize now how dysfunctional that is. But it wasn't until experiencing some things personally that were extremely painful that I had to stop and realize that the pace was costing me outside of work. And God just really walked me through and helped me to see that "this is not good."

Before, I saw everything as equal. It didn't matter if it was an expense report that had a hard deadline or a desire to get some project done that didn't have a deadline. They were all urgent to me. Everything was urgent. Everything was important. I lived in the tyranny of the urgent.

I had to learn to be okay with balls dropping. And I had to learn that there are balls made of crystal and there are balls made of rubber. If it's rubber, it's okay to let it drop because it's going to be all right. Once I was able to ask, "Okay, what type of ball is this?" I could, for some weird reason, continue the thought process of saying, "If I let this rubber ball drop, it's going to be okay. It's not the end of the world."

I had to learn that we are all going to fail, and you have to take your learnings each time you fail and get better. This whole thing is just a journey we're on. Nobody knows what they're doing. I think when you're younger, you just assume everybody knows what they're doing and you are the only one who doesn't. But as you get older, you realize, "Nope. We're all like little kids. None of us knows what we're doing. We're all trying to figure it out." So give yourself grace, give other people grace, and then be in a constant pursuit to know yourself and how God created you.[17]

EMOTIONAL INTELLIGENCE

Emotional intelligence (EQ) is the ability to recognize, understand, and manage our own emotions and then be aware of how our emotions impact other people, especially when we are experiencing stress.[18] When it comes to leadership competency, EQ has widely become recognized to be as important, if not more important, than traditional IQ (intelligence quotient) abilities.

Emotions are a big topic for women in leadership. It was woven throughout every interview, sometimes being described as an asset and part of the uniqueness that women bring to the table, and sometimes described as a liability that, if left unchecked, can hold women back from progressing in leadership.

Debbie, an executive director, said:

> I think sometimes women have had to keep the feeling part of themselves out of the equation, which is part of what makes us females. Even as "thinkers" [on a personality profile], we bring that femaleness to the equation, and it is very valuable to an organization that's supposed to be built on the love of God. But we have to help our female leaders learn the place for their emotions, because there is a place for it, but without allowing them to overwhelm their behavior.
>
> I can't tell you the number of times that I've had a woman come in my office and say, "They hurt my feelings about whatever." And I'm thinking, *Okay . . . First of all, there's no crying in baseball.* Because if you cry to a man, you will undo them. They may give you what you want momentarily, but they won't be able to really look at you and hear what you have to say. They are not trying to hurt your feelings if they disagree with you. And if you cry, or if you shirk back, or if you power down, they're going to

think that's a character or leadership flaw. Now, we know it's not, but that's what that kind of behavior in a female does to most men.

I've had to have that conversation a lot of times with a lot of young women because I don't think that they naturally know that about men. Those are the kinds of things that make the journey different between genders. I don't have any men coming to my office crying. I don't have to tell them "there's no crying in base-ball" because they already know how to play the game.[19]

Both the women and men I interviewed often talked about how passion in a man, especially around emotionally charged leadership issues, is perceived as strong, helpful, and positive. But that same passion from a woman can come across as angry, pushy, opinionated, and negative. Similarly, men who give clear instructions and expectations are thought to be good leaders, while women who do the same are often thought of as bossy.

Learning to become self-aware of one's emotions and how they impact the people around you requires hard self-examination as well as honest and clear communication from others. Self-awareness is critical to EQ and leadership, yet it is impossible to achieve without honest and empathetic feedback. We all have blind spots, but if there aren't close and trusted relationships from which to inquire and receive honest feedback, those blind spots can go unchecked and undeveloped for years.

Another common experience for a woman in a male-dominated environment is known as "personalizing," where she takes on the feeling of personal responsibility for things that are not within her control or her fault.[20] For example:

- "I couldn't make them listen to me or take my idea seriously."
- "It's my fault because I let him bully me into taking on the project."

- "My team didn't meet the goal in time. I stayed up all night feeling just terrible."

This dynamic works directly against emotional independence, assertiveness, emotional expression, stress tolerance, and flexibility, which are all qualities of healthy emotional intelligence.[21] Incorporating these attributes into your leadership and spiritual development programs will help build emotionally and spiritually healthy leaders in the context of mature and productive real-time feedback.

RELATIONSHIPS AND BIBLICAL COMMUNITY

All our leadership skill sets are just theory until they have a chance to be tried, tested, and refined when used with real people in the context of a real community. This is where the rubber meets the road, and it is a critical process in the development of a spiritual leader. Dr. Henry Cloud said, "To be truly biblical as well as truly effective, the growth process must include the Body of Christ."[22]

Most of the interviewed leaders talked about the incredible people who believed in them, gave them opportunities way before they were probably ready, and made space for mistakes and learning as a positive aspect of leading. When the community of the team, and even the whole church, also had this same "learning mind-set," the experiences were even better.

But initiating and maintaining healthy relationships are skill sets that most leaders have to develop over time and in the context of a loving and supportive community. And it's often clunky. Misunderstandings, disagreements, hurt feelings, insecurities, power struggles, jumping to conclusions, and our general sin natures tend to get the better of us. Learning how to communicate, work through conflict, listen well, empathize, and genuinely care for others are all keys to participating in and leading healthy communities. "People don't grow where they're planted; they grow where they're loved," says author Bob Goff.[23]

For example, when it comes to communication patterns, men and women—either by nature or nurture—speak differently and, without taking time to understand the differences, can easily misunderstand one other. When listening to another person, women tend to give many cues that they are paying attention and "tracking" with what is being said. Cues include engaged eye contact, smiling, nodding consistently, and soft verbal affirmations such as "uh-huh," "yes," and "gotcha." Men, on the other hand, tend to give minimal cues while listening. They may stop eye contact in order to look away and concentrate on what the person is saying. They rarely nod or give verbal affirmation.

As you can imagine, this can create a lot of misunderstandings. When a man is explaining something and a woman nods and offers a "yes," he will automatically take that as agreement when, in fact, she is just communicating that she comprehends what he is saying; her response does not necessarily mean she agrees with him. He might just move on after finishing talking and never actually ask or confirm her opinion because to him she has clearly told him she agrees; all the while she's left wondering why she didn't have an opportunity to voice her thoughts on the issue.

On the other hand, as a woman is speaking, she will often misunderstand a man's lack of eye contact and stoic facial expressions as a message that he doesn't care about what she is saying or that he isn't listening. This will often cause her to talk more or feel the need to make her case stronger with even more details and data. Or she might pull back and not give her full viewpoint because she thinks he is not tracking with what she is saying. Neither of these situations allows for every leader's thoughts to be fully expressed and evaluated.[24] Executive director Debbie said, "It takes women a while to learn how to communicate in a way that doesn't make men shut down. So if men really want the very best from the women God has brought to the table, then they have to listen."[25]

Another common experience, especially among leaders, is interrupting one another in meetings and discussions. This happens with both men and women, but for very different reasons. Men tend to interrupt to gain control over the dialogue or to turn the conversation in a specific direction. Women, on the other hand, tend to interrupt to create connection and confirm understanding. She might interject with a similar experience that affirms the point or lets you know she understands your perspective and can relate to it. Being aware of these tendencies, as well as establishing good communal communication practices, are all important in creating a supportive and helpful community in which to raise up leaders.[26]

Communication, along with the other key topics of relationships and community life, such as conflict resolution, authenticity, accountability, and expressing Christlike love to one another, are all aspects of discipleship and leadership that must be lived out and grown within a healthy and diverse faith community. As Peter Scazzero wrote, "Mature spiritual leadership is forged in the crucible of difficult conversations, the pressure of conflicted relationships, the pain of setbacks, and dark nights of the soul."[27]

In addition, most of the female leaders I interviewed talked about a significant personal and spiritual epiphany: the realization that they can't do it all, so they had to choose where to intentionally invest their time and energy, and then let go of the rest no matter who it disappoints.

This is easier for some than for others, and circumstances play a big role in how smoothly this lesson is learned. But those who had leaders who also *pastored* them through this important spiritual and leadership milestone came out on the other side stronger and more committed to ministry and their leadership than ever. "My leaders saved me from me," said Kem Meyer, a former ministry director.[28]

Integrating spiritual growth and leadership development is a critical component of developing healthy, strong, and capable female leaders within your church. A woman cannot lead from a healthy soul if we do not help integrate her relationship with Christ with the gifts and calling He has given her. "Lest," in the words of Parker Palmer, "the act of leadership do more harm than good."[29] Dr. Henry Cloud wrote, "Spiritual growth should affect relationship problems, emotional problems, and all other problems of life. There is no such thing as our 'spiritual life' and then our 'real life.' It is all one."[30]

Best Practice #5

BE AN "OTHER"

I was not exactly sure what had gone wrong. Maybe it was working too late the night before at the hospital. Perhaps I did not rehearse as much as I usually do. Or possibly, regardless of my servant-hearted intentions, volunteering to also set up chairs that Sunday morning before the performance was more than my brain could handle.

But there I was. Onstage. All alone.

What seemed like a thousand people were staring blankly at me. That familiar but disdained awkward silence filled the theater-turned-sanctuary. This was back in the day when church dramas were cutting-edge, and my mind had gone totally blank. I had performed monologues like this for church and other venues dozens of times. I knew my blocking and I knew my audience, but apparently I did not know my lines.

I backed up and started again.

Nope.

Same spot. Same word . . . nothing.

I tried it again. This time it wasn't awkward silence as much as it was uncomfortable shifting, soft whispers, and pity-filled smiles. I wanted to die, or at least escape.

But that third time was a charm. My brain unlocked. I am confident it was because the entire room was praying for me, even the people who had never prayed before. The rest of the performance spilled out of me with a combination of relief and frustration. I was grateful, because I was pretty sure actors do not get four tries. At that point, one should just shift out of the spotlight, walk off the dark stage, and quietly drive away, never to be seen again. "Oh well," I told myself. "At least people know you don't have to be perfect to be a part of this church."

But in my heart I was not as convinced. Mistakes are not easy for me. I like to do things well. Okay, let's be honest. I *love* to do things *awesomely*. And anything less than that can easily get translated in my mind as "failure," especially when I was in my early twenties.

I'd probably still be stuck in that mind-set if it weren't for people like Bob.

Bob was a small-business owner who also volunteered at our church as the weekend producer and technical director. He was the one who cast me in the monologue, and he was the first one I went to find after the service.

As usual, Bob was onstage with his headset on, directing the packing up of equipment and thanking volunteers for serving. As I started up the side steps, he caught me out of the corner of his eye. Everything else stopped. He turned to face me; smiled with that big, understanding smile of his; and stretched out his arms in the biggest fatherly hug possible.

"Girl," he said as he continued smiling and shook his head from side to side, "I am *so proud* of you. It happens to all of us, and you did *exactly* what you were supposed to do. Way. To. Go."

If you have ever received the gift of a redeeming moment like this, you know what it feels like. There's still disappointment. There's still embarrassment. There's still regret. But somehow you know you are going to be okay. And there is even a little hope that one day you will look back on this and be able to laugh about it, perhaps even appreciating the lessons you learned.

That's the way I felt in that moment and as we debriefed afterward. By the time I left my chat with Bob, I was holding my head up high and feeling good about myself again. As Dr. Henry Cloud explains in his book *The Power of the Other*, that had very little to do with me and any sort of "inner strength" I had developed as a young adult. It had everything to do with Bob, the relationship he had established with me before that fatal day, and the support and love he gave me during and afterward. Bob and I went on to produce many more incredible church services together, and he even spoke at my wedding.

Dr. Cloud explained it like this:

> Wisdom and competency do matter. We do need new skills, knowledge, and ability. . . . But . . . ask many people about their greatest accomplishment and challenges overcome, and you will find one thing in common: there was someone on the other end who made it possible.
>
> Both your best and worst seasons were not just about the market or the business cycle, or even your own skills. Your best and worst seasons were also about *who* was in that season with you. Either for good or bad. It was not just about you. It was about the others who were playing a big part in whom you were becoming and how you were doing.[1]

He went on to write that neuroscience has proven what many people have been experiencing, that it is the *relationship* that makes the difference. That is the curative factor not only in whether or not a counselor is successful with a client, but it is also the catalytic factor in a business partner, a spouse, a mentor, a pastor, or a teacher. It is the type and quality of the interpersonal connection that allows our minds to grow, expand, become stronger, and eventually succeed in reaching our goals. Relationships literally rewire our brains for better or worse. In healthy, supportive, positive relationships, our brains develop new capacities and new ways of thinking, and we are able to achieve higher levels of performance. But to perform better, you have to actually *become* better. And that can, based on neuroscience, *only* happen in the context of truly connected relationships.[2]

Although a couple of the high-level female leaders I interviewed mentioned a book or training program that helped along the way, every one talked about the critical relationships on their development journey that made the biggest impact, from either their marketplace or ministry work. Both men and women leaders had taken a personal interest in them, in their development and their achievements. These women felt as if they had a champion—someone who believed in them and saw what they were capable of doing, often before they recognized it for themselves. They also talked about the value of that friendship even after they didn't work together anymore. Sometimes they still call these people, years later, for connection, advice, and support. It is the *relationship* that makes the biggest difference.

Sherry Surratt, executive director at Orange Ministries, former CEO of MOPS, and former executive pastor at Seacoast Church, described two of the key leadership relationships that influenced her development as a leader:

> When I was at Seacoast, I worked directly for Mac Lake, who now, of course, everyone wants to hear from about leadership development. But he would often have conversations with me about what motivates people and what doesn't. How do I model good leadership? How can I help someone else model good leadership?

I learned not only to study my own leadership but to also study other people's leadership and learn from watching and imitating them. He helped me think through that and talked me through my own development and ideas about leadership.

Another person that I learned a lot from was Greg Ligon at Leadership Network, and it was in the context of developing something new. We were taking the principles we already knew, but developing a whole different experience and strategy from them. I remember being challenged by Greg as we were creating entirely new ways of facilitation and different exercises. I would have moments when I would think, *This is too big for me! I can't do this. It's too stinking big for me.* And I remember him saying to me numerous times, "Why in the world not?" which is an incredible thing to say to a young woman leader because then I would say that to myself. *Why can't I do that? Why do I think I can't do that? Of course I can do that!* It was just a huge confidence builder. Greg taught me the power of trying things and not gauging their success only on if they worked or not; he really taught me what the basis of innovation is, and I still use all that. I'm so grateful for both of these incredible leaders in my life, and when we get together, we still really enjoy catching up.[3]

In conversations with female leaders, three primary types of relationships emerged that played the biggest roles in developing female leaders:

- male mentors
- male sponsors
- female coaches

Although the roles of mentor, sponsor, and coach can be similar and overlap, especially in smaller staff settings, they have distinct and important differences that all leaders need. Because women and other minorities tend to miss out on these more relational and organic development opportunities, if you are a male church leader, it is especially important to ask yourself, "Where might I be missing opportunities to develop women in these ways?" Or, "Am I offering this to the men I lead, but not the women?"

MALE MENTORS

Mentoring relationships are usually voluntary on both sides and happen when leaders who are further along in their leadership, career, or life take time to advise, guide, and support someone who will benefit from their experience. Although the term *mentor* is often used in the church to connote spiritual mentoring, for the sake of this conversation, I am using mentoring to refer to professional and leadership development, though it can also touch on aspects of personal and spiritual development, as they are interconnected. One female leader said, "The most important thing the church did to develop me as a leader was to . . . put me in positions that stretched me as a leader and simultaneously mentored me through it all. I was never left out on my own through major growth times."[4]

Mentoring focuses on advising the individual and helping that person grow and develop through modeling, shadowing, exposure, feedback, resources, and development-oriented conversations. Research from the Center for Talent Innovation (CTI) shows that the majority of women (85 percent) and multicultural professionals (81 percent) need extra help navigating the "unwritten rules" of an organization because most of these are "caught" through informal conversations rather than learned through formal training.[5] Mentors bridge that gap by helping to reveal "the business behind the business," how to get things done, and the pitfalls to avoid, as well as offering honest feedback in a supportive way.

One survey participant stated:

> I appreciate that my church took a chance on me. My church does not have other female leaders in the role I am in, and to say that has been a struggle is an understatement. However, my mentor and boss believed me and has helped me through the struggles by being completely honest, even if it hurt. I would say the most helpful thing my mentor did for me as a growing leader, and continues to do, is to be honest. And my church has given me grace to try things, fail, and then try again.[6]

In most organizations, mentoring is an organic connection that is grown and developed through affinity and ease of relationships. Obviously, if most of the senior leaders are men, their most natural and organic connections will likely be with other men. These organic connections are called "informal networks" and often have more power within an organization than even formal lines of authority and financial resources.[7] It is often difficult for women to gain access to these informal networks. One survey participant noted the reality for many women trying to advance in their leadership skills:

> Unfortunately, the bottom line is this: men mentor men. Therefore, they choose men to push forward on the path of leadership. Since they are the ones leading, men continue to put men in traditional leadership roles. Women mentor women, thus pushing them forward in motherhood, or women's ministry, or other areas of service that women traditionally perform. With this model, the status quo will never change.[8]

But men in higher-level leadership roles can have a huge impact on developing female leaders when they choose to invite women into these informal networks, build mentoring relationships, and help them become more connected with other organizational leaders.[9] The *Harvard Business Review* noted, "From previous research, we already know that these 'male champions' genuinely believe in fairness, gender equity, and the development of talent in their organizations, and that they are easily identified by female leaders for the critical role they play advancing women's careers."[10]

Another key concept to remember when mentoring women is the "missing 33 percent." As leaders move up within an organization, their future opportunities begin to rely more on one's perceived ability to lead the organization, not just lead people. There are three primary categories of leadership: (1) your personal expertise, (2) bringing out the best in others, and (3) business, strategic, and financial acumen. For women, that last one-third (or 33 percent) is often grossly undeveloped.

In her research on this topic, Susan Colantuono found that most male mentors believed knowing the strategic and financial side of the business was a given. However, almost none of the females in their organizations knew this was a critical factor in advancement. In Colantuono's experience, talent pipelines and performance systems in organizations focus three to one on the first two elements and almost nothing on the last one. One of her male clients confessed, "I had two protégés—a man and a woman. I helped the woman build confidence and the man learn the business . . . I didn't realize I was treating them any differently!"[11]

When I was new into my executive director role overseeing all our multisite campuses, I attended my first construction meeting for a facility project we were about to begin at our biggest campus. I remember sitting in the room with architects, construction foremen, engineers, city planners, and several other male professionals. My founding pastor walked over next to me and laid out the blueprints for everyone to start working on. He posed a few questions to the group and then sat down, leaned toward me, and started explaining to me what was going on.

"This is the most important meeting of any project," he whispered as he pointed around the room. "You have to get the designers and the builders to talk to each other before you start building. It might take a while to get them on the same page, but you have to get them going because they won't do it on their own." We sat there, mostly observing, for over two hours. He would chime in on their conversation every once in a while, but it was his presence that was demanding resolution, and this group of guys clearly knew they were not leaving until there was consensus on the plan.

I will be forever grateful for the extra mentoring he gave me that day. He opened my eyes to a whole side of ministry leadership I had not experienced before, but one that would be critical to leading the launch of future campuses. But more importantly, he communicated that he saw *me* running this kind of meeting one day. I could begin to see myself leading in new areas that I had never considered before.

Other capacities that are important for emerging leaders to learn about in ministry include strategic planning, fund-raising, finance/budgets, vision casting, community relations, volunteer team building, biblical literacy, theological accuracy, and public speaking/preaching. In my experience, every church has a slightly different set of skills that qualify as "a given," so be sure to take a close look at what your actual competency expectations are for rising leaders and make sure you are explaining this to women and helping them master those competencies.

MALE SPONSORSHIP

Sponsorship is a newly named component of professional development, and awareness has been raised about the topic as more research has been done on the advantages that men have through informal networking.

If mentorship is about advice, sponsorship is about action. A sponsor helps open up organizational doors, advocates for opportunities, connects you with influential leaders inside and outside the organization, and provides cover for when you hit a roadblock or make a mistake. Minorities, women, and people of color need sponsorship most, at every career transition point—from entry level to manager, from manager to director, and so forth. Sponsors can often be a long-term relationship that lasts over the course of a career and assists at all levels of the leadership journey. "Mentors *give*, whereas sponsors *invest*. . . . Their chief role is to develop you as a leader."[12]

There are three primary ways sponsors help in your organizational advancement: pay raises, high-profile assignments, and promotions. Asking for a raise and negotiating salaries are always daunting tasks, and women are four times less likely to ask for a raise, even though they earn an average of 22 percent less than men for the same jobs.[13] However, with a sponsor cheering them on, nearly half of men and 38 percent of women will make the request, and usually get the raise according to research from the Center for Talent Innovation.[14] The same goes for asking to be assigned to a high-visibility team or a strategic project, which has proven to be critical in leadership advancement.

Sponsorship, like mentorship, can be initiated from either side of the relationship, but finding the right match is key. When a good match is found, both the sponsor and the protégé report an increase in job satisfaction and the rate of career advancement. Minority employees who have a sponsor are 65 percent more likely than their unsponsored peers to be satisfied with their rate of advancement.[15]

Jerry Hurley serves on the directional leadership team at Life. Church and is responsible for team and cultural development. During our interview, he described engaging high-capacity female leaders as a "competitive advantage" he first learned while working in corporate human resources at Target. "I've always surrounded myself with high-capacity female leaders . . . I saw value that maybe others didn't quite see yet. I intentionally created an environment that was healthy and safe, where more energy could be spent on leading and results. I guess I realized early on that female leaders can be equally as high capacity as any male leader, and I wanted to take advantage of that."[16]

Life.Church has been working their diversity initiatives through their leadership pipeline for the past twenty years and now has seven women on their leadership team of sixteen campus and central team leaders. That's 44 percent women at virtually their highest level of leadership.

Many church leaders naturally love to sponsor young leaders and may not even notice they are doing it. Women are much less likely to be sponsored by a leader at a high level, however, usually because of the lack of females at higher levels of leadership, as well as the lack of men who regularly sponsor female leaders. Because a woman's sponsor tends to be lower in the organization, the woman leader receives fewer strategic opportunities and much less exposure, thus reinforcing the cycle of fewer women being sponsored by higher-level leaders.

Look for female leaders who are responsible and productive and add them to your sponsor list. Learn about them and where they hope to advance, and work within your networks to give them exposure and new opportunities to lead and meet people. Put their names in the hat, and advocate for their promotions. In larger organizations, you can even help develop a more formal sponsorship program or process that serves every level of your leadership pipeline. As Dr. Carolyn Gordon, an associate professor at Fuller Theological Seminary, has said, "Gender equality only happens when people are willing to do more than simply talk about it. In the twenty-first century, we've got to move past a conversation to an act of doing."[17]

FEMALE COACHING

All the female leaders I interviewed remembered at least one or two female leaders whom they looked up to and from whom they received critical coaching and advice. Many leadership lessons have nothing to do with one's gender, but there is about 10 to 15 percent of a female leader's journey that is uniquely female, including navigating a male-dominated work environment and balancing all the roles and responsibilities women have in their different seasons of life.

Bill Willits, executive director of Ministry Environments at Northpoint Community Church, explained:

> I don't see any particular leadership strengths based on gender because so much of it has to do with personal wiring and gifting that I don't think leadership is a gender issue. We have some really strong male leaders, and we have some really strong female leaders. . . . The only difference I've seen is that some of our female leaders have a hard time "turning it off" because of the multiple hats they typically wear.
>
> I'll get emails at ten thirty at night sometimes. If I start to see that I'm getting too many of those, I'll say, "Hey, I just want to make sure you are able to 'turn it off,' okay?" Because what they do, and I get it, is that from four thirty to eight o'clock, it's all about family. And then they're able to reengage if they didn't get something done. Or maybe they had a doctor's appointment with one of their kids so they're just now catching up. We get that. That's not what I'm talking about. I'm talking about if somebody hasn't put appropriate or proper boundaries in place.
>
> I think we, as church leaders, have to make sure that they're putting those in. That we are asking the right questions so that we are all in this game for the long haul, not the short term. And making sure that women aren't burning themselves out because it *is* harder, many times because of the number of hats that are being worn.[18]

Those "multiple hats" have become known as the "double shift"—women who work a full-time job for their employers and then come home to work another "shift" for their families.[19] Although women have entered the workforce in record numbers, their responsibilities at home have remained similar to those of full-time housewives from thirty years ago. The encouraging news is that men today do a larger portion of chores, household work, and parenting responsibilities than any other generation before them. Almost every interviewee commented on the practical support their husbands and others in their support systems have given them. And more than one commented on wishing she had a housewife herself!

With female leaders usually carrying 75 percent of their home life, however, there is a lot to think about and work through in terms of how to prioritize, manage, outsource, release, and ask for help.[20] In addition, many women carry the extra burden of "mental labor" of home life during the workday: Who's picking up the kids? What are our plans for the weekend? Do I need to stop at the grocery store on the way home? A female coach who has "been there, done that" is in the best position to help.

Sometimes the pressures a woman needs help with are very simple and practical, but are real nonetheless. How nice would it be to get showered and ready for the day in just fifteen minutes? Or to simply throw on the same jeans from yesterday with yet another checkered, button-down shirt? Or go for a run by myself at 5:00 a.m. in the dark through my neighborhood, and maybe wear headphones and listen to music rather than being on full alert against possible danger? Or take an Uber home after a late flight without being worried for my safety? Or ride in an elevator or walk into an empty hotel room without having to check for anything questionable?

Judy, an executive pastor, explained some of the safety concerns she has to deal with:

> When it comes to personal safety as a woman, you can't turn the tapes off . . . it's nonstop. Am I alone? Is someone following me? If

I agree to meet them at the event, will I end up being by myself in a parking garage? And it's important. I spend a lot of time talking with my college-aged daughter about where she runs, how she gets to class, and how to stay aware of her surroundings at all times.[21]

Depending on her culture or context, a woman might also feel required to spend just as much time, money, and energy on her physical appearance as she does anything else because of the status and respect this brings. One executive pastor, who normally doesn't care much about her shoes, intentionally wears heels at conferences so she can more easily look a man in the eyes and therefore engage in a better conversation. Another female leader talked about the pressure to have fashionable clothes and have her nails done frequently, which ends up taking up quite a bit of her personal budget. But if she wants to be given stage time during weekend services, she has to present the proper "look." None of these things are overwhelming in and of themselves, but they do add to the collective pressure that women feel and are constantly managing.

There are also high relational pressures for women in church leadership. Not only are relationships to be developed and maintained with a woman's supervisors, peers, and direct reports, but there is usually an expectation that she will also have strong, or at least "warm," relationships with all the women on the team, regardless of their level of leadership. One executive director stated, "I learned early on that I needed to arrive early to meetings to make connections with the secretaries. If I was running behind and rushed past them into our director's meeting, I always heard about it later from one of them. I don't remember them having this expectation from any of the men on the team."

In addition, most church environments also include an expectation that female leaders will pursue relationships with their male employees' wives, including being friends, discipling, mentoring, developing them as leaders, and "doing life together." This is rarely the case for male leaders in the church, or in any other profession. Female leaders also tend to have to carry the mantle of being available and building into relationships within the women's ministry regardless if this is within her direct oversight or not.

Unfortunately, many female leaders are reluctant to reach out for help and support because they don't want to appear "needy," they are unaware of the benefits they could receive from such a coaching relationship, or they lack the resources to find or pay for coaching. In addition, it is often difficult for a woman in ministry to find quality female leaders available who fully understand the skills and challenges of leadership in the context of a ministry setting. And then, of course, you want to find someone you actually like, respect, and want to learn from; it can feel like looking for a needle in a haystack.

As a church, supporting your female leaders at all levels of the organization with time and budget to receive leadership coaching is a wonderful, and relatively inexpensive, way to invest in their individual development and address the barriers that you may not even be aware of that are limiting their growth, progress, and job satisfaction. You can also bring in female speakers and trainers to expose your leadership team members, both men and women, to female voices and perspectives, as well as model diversity as a high value.

Being and providing quality "others" in the form of male mentors, male sponsors, and female coaches will give your female leaders the supportive connections and authentic relationships they need to learn, grow, and develop into the capable leaders your church needs and the fruitful leaders God has called them to be. May we all learn to be, and have, many "Bobs."

Best Practice #6

CREATE AN ENVIRONMENT
OF SAFETY

In my opinion, one of the biggest challenges of developing female leaders in our churches is that most of the "others" on our leadership teams are male and, in the context of this conversation, the protégés are female. A male mentor investing in growing a female leader is no small task in the church world. Besides the basic gender differences, the relational and potentially romantic tensions are real and a very big issue. We have all been affected by the heartbreaking news that a church has gone through a leadership crisis because of an inappropriate relationship. It is crushing every time for the church, the people personally involved, and the church's reputation in the community, as well as having a lifelong impact on its youth and young believers.

It is estimated that more than one-third of women have been sexually harassed or abused at work.[1] In our survey of female leaders who are currently serving in ministry roles, more than 15 percent said they had experienced inappropriate advances or treatment by a man in authority over them. Here are just some of their experiences:

- "It was the most difficult experience of my recent life. However, God did get me through."
- "Gaslighting, belittling, yelling, and screaming were some of the emotional and verbal abuse I received."
- "The senior pastor of the first church I was on staff with was eventually exposed as having an affair with the worship leader. I often felt uncomfortable with the intimate way he spoke to me. I was naive and confused by his attention."
- "As a single woman, I was treated as something to be feared, that I was out to find a man at all costs. I would like to be married and have a family, but it is not my all-consuming call. Many of my male colleagues did not see it that way and treated me accordingly. They feared me instead of seeing me as equally gifted and useful in ministry."
- "The senior pastor made an inappropriate comment about my chest. There was no place I could report him."
- "I have had male leaders over me who have had feelings for me. I was in youth group and they were both the assistant youth leaders in their twenties. I was super young and actually kind of liked them because I thought they were godly men. So I fell into the trap twice. It never got to the point where I was actually intimate with them, but they would text me all the time and try to spend time with me outside of youth group. It broke my heart when it did not end up working out with the first guy, and I got blamed for the whole relationship. I ended it with the second guy, and he thanked me for doing so. He knew it wasn't right

and still went along with it. Neither of these guys did anything inappropriate for relationship standards outside of the church. I believe they actually did like me. They just overstepped their boundaries. It made everything very confusing and quite honestly made me want to leave that church."

- "I was belittled, put down, my ideas were mocked, and I was betrayed. He even said that I needed to just 'take it.'"
- "I was called 'little girl' and treated paternalistically by other leaders in group settings. I was left out of ministry and theology conversations. Rude comments were made about my dress, age, hair, cuteness, and so forth."
- "I was removed from a position due to jealousy and a perceived relationship with a man in leadership, which was not the case. The man remained in place."
- "I've literally been told to 'just go on stage and look pretty for everybody.'"[2]

It is heartbreaking to read these stories. These are our sisters in Christ who, because they trusted their leaders and wanted to protect their church, often let down their guard, covered over inappropriate behavior, took the blame, or stayed silent. From belittling to full-on sexual harassment and assault, none of these behaviors are acceptable in the family of God.

But this fear is not only in churches. With the significant rise in sex scandals and harassment charges, male leaders in industries everywhere are rethinking their professional practices, and some are intentionally limiting their one-on-one meetings with women.[3] The #MeToo and #ChurchToo movements have come a long way in raising awareness, giving survivors a voice, and holding those in authority accountable for inappropriate, unethical, illegal, and downright disgusting behaviors.

One of the things I appreciate most about being involved in

church ministry is that, as Christians, we *know* this is wrong. Taking advantage of women, abusing leadership authority, and intimate relationships—both physical and emotional—outside of marriage are clearly against how God instructs us to live and have absolutely no place in a Christian leader's life. Our job as church leaders is the opposite—we are to protect, defend, and bring freedom. And we are to quickly expose any leader who is violating those standards.

However, I also know that it is very difficult to adequately blend together our calling to personal purity, our calling as leaders to develop others, and the reality that we are all sinful people living in a broken world. How does a male pastor honor God by mentoring and developing female leaders and yet also honor God by protecting himself, his marriage, and his ministry from universal, fleshly, and very real temptations?

This is a very tough question. To be honest, I know I do not have the full answer, or even a full perspective. But to avoid the topic or to not, at the very least, try to help catalyze our collective conversation would be a disservice to the gifted women in our churches and the proactive leaders who are trying to do a better job navigating these landmines.

I am thankful and humbled to be able to say that I have never had a spiritual leader treat me in a deliberately inappropriate way, try to make any sexual advances toward me, or even cause me to be fearful, concerned, or uncomfortable. Not that there haven't been some awkward moments along the way, but overall I have worked with gentlemen and have felt physically, emotionally, and spiritually safe. I believe I owe a lot of this to the now controversial "Billy Graham Rules."

The Billy Graham Rules didn't start out with that name, nor did they have anything to do with women working in church leadership. They were originally part of the "Modesto Manifesto," which Billy Graham described in his autobiography, *Just As I Am*.[4] In 1948,

Billy Graham and his team were in the beginning stages of their evangelistic ministry and were staying in Modesto, California, for two weeks of citywide revival meetings. They had been talking as a team about the poor reputation of large-scale evangelism, especially portrayed in the media. As they discussed some of the critiques, they had to admit that some of the evangelists of the time were guilty of these ungodly behaviors. Billy asked the team members to take the next hour to go to their own rooms and brainstorm all the things they saw their peers doing that were discrediting their ministries. When they came back together, they found that their lists were almost identical. They combined their thoughts and concerns, and developed four commitments they made to one another to keep from falling into these disparaging traps.

1. *Money:* The team agreed not to pressure people to give financially through "love offerings" that would in any way tempt them to emotionally or spiritually manipulate people for funding, and they agreed to create high accountability for all finances. As much as possible, all their funding would be raised by local committees in advance of their meetings, and they would never make emotional pleas for donations.

2. *Dangers of Sexual Immorality:* This issue was of particular importance because of their extensive travel schedule at a time when there was little communication possible with their wives and families. There had been several instances of evangelists who had fallen into immorality, and they didn't want to give even the appearance of compromise or suspicion *to the media* while on the road. They all agreed to no longer travel, meet, or eat alone with a woman other than their wives so the media wouldn't have any opportunity to assume the worst.

3. *Uphold the Local Church:* There was a tendency for evangelists to carry on their ministry apart from local churches

and to even criticize local church leaders. Billy Graham and his team found this to be unbiblical and created their entire strategy around engaging and supporting local churches in partnerships together for the gospel.

4. *Publicity:* Billy Graham's team had seen many evangelists exaggerate their attendance and response numbers in an effort to gain more publicity. Unfortunately, this discredited them with the press, who were also at the events. So this team decided that they would be scrupulous in their reporting and publicity efforts.

I love this list. To be honest, I wish more pastors had adopted all four points, not just number two. It is amazing the legacy one leaves when integrity in all aspects of life and leadership is at the top of their priority list. *Integrity* is the word I would use to describe my pastors when I worked at Christ Fellowship Church, and as an employee and a church member, that integrity was palpable.

Our lead pastors often taught at staff meetings about the importance of personal purity and of pursuing holiness at an individual level. They often emphasized to our team and volunteer leaders that our rapid growth and ministry "success" were not based on us but simply on God's choice to put His hand of grace on us, and that any of us had the power to violate that trust and therefore stall what God was doing in our region.

My direct supervisor at Christ Fellowship was Pastor Todd Mullins. At the time, Todd was the worship pastor and executive pastor of our fast-growing church. One of my earliest memories of his trustworthy integrity was when, as a new church member, I volunteered as the producer for our first live worship recording.

Several of us had met at the mall to make purchases for the production, and Todd came because he was the only one with a church credit card. As we walked the mall, every time we passed by the Victoria's

Secret store, he would look down. At first I didn't think anything of it, but after it happened two or three times that afternoon, I started to realize he was intentionally looking away from the scantily clad models in the window displays. He didn't say anything, he didn't make a big deal of it, and he wasn't even doing it to impress any of us. I saw him do it one time walking all by himself when he didn't know anyone was looking. It was a part of his personal commitment to purity. And that personal commitment he made played out in hundreds of God-honoring ways in my working relationship with him.

We had a great working relationship that involved connection, friendship, chemistry, disagreement, problem-solving, celebration moments, low points of frustration, and lots of hard work. But not one time did he ever make me feel personally uncomfortable, cross an inappropriate boundary in conversation or actions, or cause me to wonder if that would ever be an issue. I don't think there is a way to adequately describe the leadership gift it is to feel safe with your leader. He didn't say I was safe; his personal commitment to the Lord and his pursuit of daily holiness naturally gave me the gift of freedom to work and lead without concern.

Because our church was so committed to integrity and personal purity, we implemented many of the standard Billy Graham Rules components: a glass window in every office door, not traveling alone with someone of the opposite sex, and safeguards on our computers. However, I believe the problem with the Billy Graham Rules is that, in the context of all we do in ministry today, they don't go far *enough* or in the right *ways*. Here is why.

WE LIVE IN A DIFFERENT TIME

I have served for the last twenty years under this rule, and, as I said before, I am very appreciative of its boundaries and protections.

However, we do not live in 1948 anymore. I think the Modesto Manifesto was an incredible step of faithfulness and maturity and was exactly what was needed at that time, for that ministry, and in that era. But we live in a very different time.

The last few churches I have consulted with that lost a high-level leader to sexual immorality had all the typical BG Rules in place. Instead, these leaders built inappropriate relationships over text messages, cell phone calls, or using personal email accounts that were hidden from the church and their spouses. When the heart wants to wander, it will find a way. And in today's technology-saturated world, it is not hard to start and maintain a double life, sometimes for months and even years.

In addition, in 1948 almost everyone married very young, so the guidelines tend to rely on the accountability of a spouse. It does not give much guidance or wisdom to leaders who are single, which is much more common today.

WE LIVE IN A DIFFERENT CULTURE

Gone are the days when men meeting with men and women meeting with women is above reproach. When I was in college, I was a resident assistant in the freshman, all-girls dorm. Partway into the year, I learned that one of the girls on my floor was a lesbian and that she had feelings for me. In our typical church mind-set, a dorm full of girls seems completely "safe." But we live in a culture where LGBTQ is commonplace now. A senior pastor traveling with a young seminary intern is no longer "without suspicion," especially if just the two of them are traveling together, eating together, and sharing a room together. In today's culture, I would consider that quite suspicious. It's time to think about these boundaries differently.

MANY PEOPLE DON'T UNDERSTAND APPROPRIATE LEVELS OF RELATIONAL INTIMACY

The more postmodern our society gets and the more unstable the families in which we are raised become, the more confused we are about what healthy relationships are, particularly around the topic of intimacy.

I've seen several really good frameworks for teaching on levels of relationships, but my favorite comes from Joseph Myers's book *The Search to Belong*, where he outlines four levels of community. He not only describes the characteristics of each of these types of relationships but suggests physical space boundaries that should match the level of emotional connection.

We need all four of these types of relationships, but in different quantities. The less connected the relationship, the greater number of them we need. The more connected and intimate, the fewer. Unfortunately, often in church ministry we tend to hyperfocus on intimacy and underplay the need for more social connections. This sets up our leaders and our congregation to violate these healthy levels of intimacy and walk down a sinful path. Here is a quick summary of Myers's concept and how we can apply this to developing female leaders in our churches:

1. *Public Space: twelve feet apart.* These are the most common relationships we have and are full of a sense of connection and togetherness, even though we might not know each other well. Our conversations often center on basic, "safe" topics, and we give each other lots of space to be ourselves. We might shake hands every once in a while, but for the most part, these are people we see and talk to but don't often enter

into each other's personal spaces. Fellow church members are an example of public relationships.

2. *Social Space: twelve to four feet apart.* These are "neighbor"-type relationships. We know these people, we know about them, and we are connected, but we are still able to decide which parts of ourselves we reveal, how we reveal them, and how much we want to reveal. Social relationships are often undervalued in churches because they can seem to stay only on the "surface" and not grow to be spiritually serious enough. However, social relationships are incredibly important for emotional health and make up a big portion of our support network. Just like a good neighbor, this is the person you will feel free to ask a favor of and be glad when you are able to return the favor. These are our friends. We stand or sit close enough for personal conversations, or we might give the occasional hug at church. Most relationships should stop at this level and provide a lifetime of mutually enjoyable moments, supportive care, and special memories.

3. *Personal Space: four feet to eighteen inches apart.* These are our close friends, people we would consider "family." These are often the types of relationships that churches define as "community" or "doing life together." I like the description of "refrigerator rights"—the type of relationships where we can walk into each other's houses and grab something to drink out of the fridge without anyone feeling like that is strange. The challenge with these personal relationships is that much of our church language describes these kinds of relationships as "intimate," "vulnerable," and "transparent."

Although there is a level of vulnerability in trusted friendships, full exposure should be reserved only for truly intimate relationships. Not being able to develop or maintain social space friendships is often a sign of emotional or relational unhealthiness. This can involve either not knowing how to maintain appropriate levels of close conversation or inappropriately inviting intimacy levels into social space friendships.

There is often pressure for church staff members to have this kind of personal connection if they work together. They feel they must "do life together" or "want to hang out together" to be productive teammates. I think this creates unnecessary pressure on teams and relationships, and it sets up our working dynamics to "feel less," even though we are being very effective for our churches. This expectation also works against creating healthy male-female working relationships because this will naturally apply unnecessary pressure to connect when we are also trying to protect purity.

4. *Intimate Space: eighteen to zero inches.* These are our deepest and closest intimate relationships. Very few relationships are intimate over the course of our lifetimes. These are the spaces in which we are "naked" and yet "not ashamed." Marriage is one. A mother and baby is another. It is not only physical nakedness, but emotional, informational, and spatial.

In a medical situation, there may be physical exposure but there is not any shame because it does not involve sexuality or other aspects of intimacy, such as shared emotional intimacy. The assumption in many of our Christian communities is that intimacy is the goal and that relationships should be continually moving toward more intimacy. But that is not healthy. Very few relationships should get to this point. And a designated intimate relationship, such as a marriage, should not stop short of full intimacy. Intimate relationships are also exclusively one-on-one, whereas the previous types of relationships are free to have others participate. When we spend too much time nurturing one-on-one relationships in places where we shouldn't, we naturally build levels of intimacy that can't be shared with everyone on our teams.[5]

As you can see, there are plenty of opportunities for healthy male-female relationships on our teams in the public, social, and personal spaces. The key is to not only teach our leaders about guidelines of when we can be alone with someone else—which, in my opinion, are not concrete enough in our age of technology—but to go *further* by also teaching about levels of emotional, spiritual, intellectual, and physical intimacy and how to ensure everyone has the appropriate number of relationships in the correct categories. When we are off-balance, such as having too many intimate or not enough social relationships, we end up trying to fill our needs with the wrong relationship, our judgment is clouded by our unmet needs, and we walk down paths we never thought we would find ourselves on.

When we are talking about male leaders intentionally investing in the development of female leaders, I see sponsorship as a public relationship (twelve feet apart), mentoring as a social relationship (twelve to four feet apart), and coaching as a personal relationship (four feet to eighteen inches apart), which is why I think female leaders receiving coaching from an experienced female ministry leader is best. There are often aspects of one's personal life, family, relationships, and spiritual growth that require this type of closer connection to address. The key is for male leaders to make sure their team members have all these types of relationships with someone and that each of their team members receives the same development. For example, a male ministry leader can be very intentional and still appropriate in his leadership development efforts if he does three things:

- mentors all his team equally by developing his leaders in ways that can be done for both men and women;
- intentionally sponsors leaders throughout his organization,

with a goal that 50 percent of them are female or other minorities; and
- uses his budget to pay for additional coaching for each of his team members.

Undergoing efforts like these provides well-rounded development for everyone on your team, encourages investment in other up-and-coming leaders throughout the church, and minimizes discrimination or unintended biases.

Dr. Karen Longman is a professor and program director of higher education at Azusa Pacific University as well as a senior fellow with the Council for Christian Colleges & Universities (CCCU), where she has coordinated Leadership Development Institutes for emerging leaders within the CCCU since 1998. She has long been an advocate for building strong mentoring relationships with both men and women. "Relationships don't get stigmatized if you have a lot of them," she explains, "so lunch vigorously."[6]

Many have forgotten that discipleship and leadership are not the same thing. I know it can get confusing when we are working in church ministry, but I've found that if we don't distinguish between the two, at least on some levels, it can lead our team members to apply the wrong types of connection in the wrong situations.

In discipleship relationships, we are all equal. There is true community. We are all sinners, and no one person is better than anyone else. We are all equal at the foot of the cross. We are called to love one another, serve one another, bear one another's burdens, be at peace with one another, and speak the truth to one another, along with ninety-five other "one another" commands. I love the "one anothers." I resonate with their sense of community and oneness in Christ.

But leadership is very different. Although we are still called to love and serve as leaders, there is a shift in authority and power. You can never truly be in an equal relationship when one person holds more power than the other person. In my opinion, this is why some of the men being accused in the #MeToo movement are surprised by the response to their actions; they forgot that they automatically had more power than the people they abused. Full "mutual consent" is not possible when there is authority involved. It doesn't matter if you overtly leverage it or not; power is still part of the relationship.

Parenting is a similar dynamic. My son and I can have a very close and mutually loving relationship, but at the end of the day, I am still the parent and I control his resources and potential, and can even choose to manipulate his emotions and understanding of how the world works. We will never have a fully equal connection. It is on me, as the parent, to steward that and take responsibility for its implications.

When a leader holds authority through a position as a spiritual leader or as an employer, that authority will always be a part of the relationship. Trying to "flip" into a discipleship connection is not only inappropriate, it is impossible. In my opinion, this is one of the primary reasons God outlines requirements for leadership in the Bible. One has to be able to navigate authority in relationships well to lead in a healthy way in the church.

In my early twenties, I was a registered nurse and worked in a locked psychiatric unit at the veterans hospital. Boundaries are incredibly important in health care, particularly in this type of setting. We regularly utilized a concept called "therapeutic use of self."[7] It's the professional ability of a health care provider to establish and maintain a relationship of trust that facilitates positive patient outcomes. The relationship is built on five components: trust, respect, empathy, professional intimacy, and appropriate use of power inherent in the care provider's role. For trust, respect, and empathy, in particular, a nurse or other health care provider has to be able and willing to be relationally connected and appropriately emotionally vulnerable. But the goal is not for the nurse to feel a connection. Rather, the goal is for the nurse to utilize his or her own life experiences and interpersonal relationship skills in an *authentic* yet *emotionally neutral* way that facilitates healing for the patient and maintains professional objectivity for the nurse.

In my experience, few ministry leaders have been taught these types of professional boundaries. In order to create a trusting, open, and relational environment, they enter into a discipleship-type relationship with the parishioner or subordinate in which appropriate boundaries are easily violated, or at the very least, easily misunderstood. Knowing the differences between who I am called to be as a *disciple* and how I need to serve others as a *leader* is a key element in fostering healthy, appropriate, and God-honoring relationships.

What should we do?

As I said before, I certainly do not have all the answers, but I recently spent some time in a roundtable discussion about this topic with a group of senior pastors. Here are the suggestions I gave them to begin to lean in to this topic and create better professional practices that not only protect leaders and their churches but create healthy spaces to develop leaders of all kinds. I hope they are helpful to you as well.

1. ALWAYS TAKE TWO

A leadership development concept that I love is "always take someone with you." It basically challenges all of us to bring someone along in development as we go about our leadership. If you are headed to the hospital to visit someone, don't waste the opportunity. Take a younger leader along with you, talk on the way, explain how you prepare for this kind of ministry, let him or her watch you serve the family, and then debrief with that person on the way back to the office. This kind of mentoring is very powerful. Plus, the personal time invested communicates all sorts of value to an up-and-coming leader.

But I think we should expand this practice to "always take two." Two men, two women, or one man and one woman plus you makes three, and there is safety in groups of three or more. By taking *two* leaders, you instantly double your development efforts and create a safe environment at the same time. It takes away the intimacy and one-on-one exclusive connection. It not only helps connect young leaders to you personally, but it also builds peer relationships between two people who are a lot more likely to be available and stay in relationship with each other over their lifetimes. In addition, you take any pressure off anything that might look inappropriate or that hints that you might be showing favoritism based on gender.

If we were to play the movie of our culture forward twenty years, what leadership practices should you implement *now* to make sure you are being equitable to everyone and creating safe and accountable scenarios for yourself? Doubling your impact can do that. Take two people to lunch. Always bring along two additional people to a conference. Meet two people for coffee. This doesn't mean you can't still have conversations with individuals one-on-one. These are the conversations that can easily be done in your office with the appropriate boundaries already in place. But as you travel or take advantage of unique "bring someone with you" developmental opportunities, replace the private, individual, intimate connections with "take two." Your personal leadership and your church will be stronger for it.

2. REGULARLY TEACH ON PERSONAL PURITY AND SELF-LEADERSHIP

Leadership, and ministry leadership specifically, tends to be so oriented toward others that we forget it is all based on our own walk with the Lord, personal character, and integrity. We all need to be reminded of this regularly. Teach on the levels of intimacy. Talk in your teams about how to keep a pure heart and regularly challenge motives in ministry. Train your leaders about how temptation works, what God says to do about it, and what steps you expect them to take as leaders when it happens. How should they bring it into the light when it is still in the temptation phase and before the sin phase? How does this work when your job is attached to your behavior? How can you create a healthy culture where these issues are taken care of proactively before they blow up into a crisis? Our sins *will* find us out. How can you equip your leaders to prevent that from happening?

3. ESTABLISH CLEAR BOUNDARIES AND TRAIN ON PROFESSIONAL BEST PRACTICES

I think some of the practices of the Billy Graham Rules are very helpful, not because they prevent issues, but because they raise awareness and keep the conversation alive within our teams. It's kind of like having a uniformed police officer present in your children's ministry during worship services. That one person probably isn't going to deter a major security breach or a violent attack, but if someone is looking for an easy target and they see the officer, they will not come to your church. It also raises awareness of security issues for the entire congregation and keeps us from assuming just because we are in a church building we don't have to be aware of our surroundings.

Similarly, practices such as having glass windows in every office, anti-pornography software on church computers, and not meeting someone in an intimate setting—such as a private dinner, a stroll on the beach, long conversations in a parked car—are all ways we raise awareness and help leaders implement intelligent and wise personal practices. If you have a predator on your team, these guidelines are certainly not going to stop him or her. But it will deter someone who is looking for an easy opportunity and hopefully protect anyone who stumbles into a moment of weakness. It also reminds the whole team that if someone is practicing unhealthy behaviors or regularly violating your guidelines, it is their job to confront the person and raise the issue to the appropriate person on your staff team.

It should be standard practice in churches, just as it is in every other industry, to offer regular training to staff and leaders on diversity awareness and sexual harassment. It is critical that we begin talking about these issues more openly and clearly defining the professional standards to which we want to hold ourselves.

4. BE SMART ABOUT ALCOHOL AND MENTAL HEALTH

If we are going to rethink our practices, we have to be realistic about the things that can impair our judgment. Alcohol, some medications, drug use, lack of sleep, stress, and mental and emotional health issues can all "prime" us for making poor choices we wouldn't normally make. Even a small amount of alcohol (one glass of wine) has been documented to impair decision making, increase reckless behavior, and weaken memory ability.[8]

Several churches I know have outlined a "leadership covenant" that raises the bar on behaviors and standards they expect from people they have given positions of leadership, even as volunteers. It is important to explain that many of these things aren't necessarily issues of sin, but are wise given the context and mission of your church.

When it comes to drinking alcohol, I've personally agreed to these types of commitments for a variety of jobs or volunteer roles, but they've all had slightly different guidelines. In one case, I worked and lived at a Christian college in which no alcohol was allowed on campus. Then I worked at a church in which we agreed to drink only in the privacy of our own homes, but not in public. I have been part of a church in which the culture encouraged limiting alcohol to just one drink, and a church that asked us to not drink at all, in any situation. Each request had logic and wisdom behind it that I appreciated, respected, and gladly participated in. I am thankful for the wisdom my leaders lent me, especially when I think back to my early leadership years. Teaching your leaders to be smart about the freedoms they have, and why it is important to create the boundaries you are asking for, will equip them to be able to focus on the bigger work of building God's kingdom.

5. CHALLENGE YOUR ASSUMPTIONS

One of the most frustrating parts of these "rules" is that many of them, at least in today's world, simply don't make sense. According to some of the practices I lived within, I could meet with a man in my office with a skinny rectangular window for several hours undisturbed but couldn't meet in a busy coffee shop where everyone could see us and overhear our conversation. I couldn't ride in a car with a man to the airport for an early-morning flight, but we could stay in the same hotel where we had the discounted conference rate. There was fear around my leadership relationships with men I worked with and met with only one to two times a month for an hour, but their female administrative assistants had full access to their personal schedules, talked to them on the phone multiple times during the day, and were closely connected with much of their personal lives.

Again, I think many of these practices are helpful in bringing awareness, but we have to at least acknowledge that they sometimes contradict themselves and often don't make much sense and don't actually provide the protection we say they do.

And since women tend to get the short end of the stick on these guidelines, I think we need to do a better job reinventing them, teaching about them, and holding one another accountable to them. Take time to truly analyze the guidelines you are giving your team, think about unspoken assumptions that you may have adopted, and make sure that the guidelines are actually doing what you want them to do. Be sure to ask yourselves and your female leaders what the unintended consequences might be and how you can do a better job creating a safe and inclusive leadership environment for everyone.

One of the leading voices in the Christian community on rethinking how we handle interactions between men and women is John Ortberg, a well-known author and senior pastor. For more than thirty years, John has been learning how to create team environments in which female leaders can also thrive. This is how he explained his perspective to me:

At times, of course, churches or organizations may have a theology that would keep women from leading or keep female leaders from flourishing. I remember many years ago hearing a woman say, "Help, I'm a leader trapped in a woman's body!" Occasionally there may be openness theologically and organizationally, but systems get constructed that exclude women. Guys end up having recreational activities together that women may be excluded from or they may have styles, or humor, or [ways of] relating, or places they go that become, intentionally or not, exclusive.

Also, in a misguided attempt to want to keep sexual boundaries clear and honored, leaders can enter a "strategy of isolation." Sometimes you'll hear in Christian organizations male leaders who might even take pride in saying, "I'm never alone with a woman. I would never be in a car alone with a woman. I would never have a meeting alone with a woman." And, of course, the great difficulty with this is that they never try to understand what it will take to be intentional about seeking to mentor, and develop, and encourage, and breathe life into women leaders as well as men leaders.

Back in Jesus' time, the Pharisees often adopted what might be called a "strategy of isolation" to avoid sexual sin with a woman where they would not talk to a woman, or touch a woman, or even look at a woman. I do not believe a "strategy of isolation" is a good way to avoid sexual sin, and it's a terrible way to help develop a culture where women and men can serve and lead together.

At our church, we'll talk about three concrete ways to seek to keep integrity in our sexual behavior.

- *The Sibling Test:* If I'm with someone of the opposite sex, is my behavior with them the same as it would be with my sister (my sibling)?
- *The Screen Test:* When I'm with someone of the opposite sex that is not my spouse, am I saying or doing things I'd be ashamed of if they were put up on a screen for our whole congregation to see?
- *The Secret Test:* Am I keeping secrets with this person of the opposite sex that my spouse does not know about?

I've also found it helpful to ask for feedback from people who are on staff, especially from women who serve at church where I'm working, so that we can get a better grip on how our culture might help or hinder the flourishing of women in leadership.[9]

Navigating these tensions of relational connection and appropriate boundaries is a challenge for everyone in leadership. However, it is worth it. As one survey participant stated, "So far, in my church leadership journey it's been a male who has opened the door for me, believed in me, and lifted me into a position of leadership. I'm really thankful for them because they saw something in me before I believed it about myself."[10]

CREATING SAFE WORK ENVIRONMENTS

Creating a safe work environment free from harassment or predatorial behavior by anyone is imperative to the development of both male and female leaders who are godly, healthy, and trustworthy. Creating clear policies, raising awareness, offering training, and creating an "open-door" culture with clear directions on whom to talk to if someone is creating a hostile, or even uncomfortable, environment are critical in addressing these very real issues. I pray that none of our churches will have to walk down these difficult roads, but raising awareness and openly talking about what to do if it happens to your leaders will equip and empower your female (and male) leaders to know they are valued and that your church is a safe place to lead and to work.

Along with relationship boundaries that need to be in place for effective mentoring, sponsoring, and coaching, when it comes to paid employees, there are additional legal and ethical liabilities if we don't create a reasonably safe work environment, free from abuses of power or spiritual authority, harassment, insults, threats, intimidation, ridicule, assaults, mockery, and offensive environments. Keep in mind, these kinds of abuses don't only come from a direct supervisor, but can come from a leader in another area or even a volunteer or church member. According to the US Equal Employment Opportunity Commission:

> Prevention is the best tool to eliminate harassment in the workplace. Employers are encouraged to take appropriate steps to prevent and

correct unlawful harassment. They should clearly communicate to employees that unwelcome harassing conduct will not be tolerated. They can do this by establishing an effective complaint or grievance process, providing anti-harassment training to their managers and employees, and taking immediate and appropriate action when an employee complains. Employers should strive to create an environment in which employees feel free to raise concerns and are confident that those concerns will be addressed.[11]

The last point is critical and often underdeveloped in churches. If someone is experiencing inappropriate behavior, there should be a clear person and a well-known process for how complaints and accusations are handled, *no matter who the accused is*. That means there needs to be accountability and thorough follow-up provided for everyone, from a church member to the senior pastor and elders. Creating a process to handle these kinds of issues before an accusation has been made allows the church to lead well and with integrity, despite the ugliness of these types of situations.

By rethinking our practices, policies, and procedures to fit today's culture, we can create safe environments that empower women, defend the innocent, *and* protect the church.

Best Practice #7

UPGRADE YOUR
PEOPLE PRACTICES

I'm telling you I just wasn't aware at the time," explained Kem Meyer, former director of communications and a church consultant. "I was so naive. Looking back when I was working at the church, it was *years* before I realized that it is male dominated. I remember having people asking me about it and thinking, *What are you talking about? I've just got my head down, and am just doing my stuff.* Again, I simply was not thinking about it. It's only in hindsight that I see, 'Oh my gosh, it *is* male dominated.'"

Kem continued:

But I think the higher up I went in leadership, the more I could *see* the systematic gender assumptions. I could see them and started hearing about them more, even if I hadn't necessarily experienced them myself. Eventually, as I got higher in leadership, I actually started feeling them myself. It was real subtle; none of it was overt. I wasn't harassed, but it started to actually impede my ability to do my job. I hadn't experienced that before because I always had independent departments or projects to run where I had a playground that, if I was experiencing roadblocks in one area, I could focus on another area of my work and make progress there instead.

For a few years now, I've been in a place of greater maturity and reflection, and I've had more and more people challenging me and my responsibility. "Don't you understand? You're in a place that so many women can't get to. Can you please speak about these issues?" I thought, *No, I'm not going to speak about these issues just because I'm a woman.* But their constant prompting forced me to reflect and pay more attention. It made me realize the hurdles that had been cleared for me. There were people who had gone before me, and I wouldn't be able to do what I'm doing now if they hadn't stuck their necks out for me then. *That* is why I'm here.

I know now that it's my turn to stick my neck out for others because otherwise I'm just perpetuating a pattern I don't want to perpetuate.[1]

Kem wasn't the only interviewee to confess "not noticing" that she was often one of few (or the only) women at the leadership table, or that she had opportunities and benefits that weren't available to all women. In fact, many of our female leaders talked about how it took them a long time to realize that there might, in fact, be some bias going on around them. Why is this?

For one, our brains are made to notice patterns, make generalizations, and create categories. It's what helps us navigate our complex world and make sense of all the information coming at us during a given day. It makes us efficient, smart, and decisive. But it can also set us up to overgeneralize, even when we think we are doing the good or right thing. This is known as unconscious bias or implicit bias, and it shows up in real-life situations all the time.

In fact, "field experiments demonstrate that real-world discrimination continues, and is widespread. White applicants get about 50 percent more call-backs than black applicants with the same resumes; college professors are 26 percent more likely to respond to a student's email when it is signed by Brad rather than Lamar; and physicians recommend less pain medication for black patients than white patients with the same injury."[2] Obviously, no doctor wants to under-medicate an injured person, but he or she may do it without realizing it.

It is hard to admit that we have biases when we can be so blind to them. This is especially true for us as Christians when Jesus' unconditional love and mercy are central to our experience and belief system. Bias and discrimination seem to go against everything for which we live. However, as we look through history, it's not hard to find examples of well-meaning believers who thought they were acting in righteous and unbiased ways when they really were not.

Slavery is one practice that comes to mind. Holy wars are another. In fact, there is actually a direct correlation between how strongly we believe we do not have any bias and the amount of biased thinking and behaviors we actually exhibit.[3] It seems counterintuitive, but the more we are certain we are unbiased, the more likely we are to be very biased. We are not open to learning about our blind spots and making changes to our thinking and behavior. The key, though, is to stay open, curious, humble, and realistic. Bias is something we have all been raised with, and something we all must constantly assess in our own hearts and in the influence we steward.

There is a fear, especially for Christian women, of being labeled "feminist." In many Christian circles, the word *feminist* tends to stir up images of proabortion, bra-burning, family-hating, angry women who believe that God is female, men are worthless, and the Bible is full of errors.[4] I even remember reading an article in *Christianity Today* several years ago where *feminist* was called "The Christian F-Word."[5]

Naturally, as female leaders in the church, most of us have not been that eager to champion a woman's role or development, even our own, for fear of taking it too far. And to be honest, most of us are just grateful for the opportunity to serve and be a part of ministry. This "no-agenda" approach has been the very thing that has allowed us to be trusted to lead. To turn the tables and "play the gender card" can invoke a fear of being misunderstood or dismissed, losing our influence, or even being removed or sidelined from ministry leadership. Unfortunately, this fear has also created a cycle in which women leaders are actually helping to propagate the very systems and practices that are holding us back.

To begin to talk about our inherited tendencies toward bias, define what we really believe about a woman's role in our church, and come to grips with anything we may have done wrong in the past that we want to change for the future requires courage, humility, openness, perseverance, strength, and faith. Whether we are male or female, young or old, we are all going to have to lean in to our relationship with the Lord, dig deep into our own belief systems and learned behaviors, and be open to "owning" where we have been wrong in the past. Thankfully, our God is a master of revealing our missteps and giving us a forgiving path forward into a new way of living and loving one another.

Although there is a tendency for bias at all levels of a volunteer organization, hands down the number one topic to show up in my interviews and our survey responses was around fair and equal treatment of paid employees. In everything from recruiting practices to retirement benefits, making sure female leaders receive equal and ethical treatment for the work they contribute was an important issue, not just for women, but as a statement about how churches function as employers within our communities.

The benefit of taking a close look at our human resource practices and how we concretely treat employees is that we don't have to rely on just our own self-awareness or the ability of others to clearly communicate their subjective experiences. Much of what we can look at to assess our unconscious biases and hold ourselves accountable is in black and white. Facing the reality of how we recruit and hire, pay and support, and develop and assess both our male and female workers can give us unique insight into our culture's blind spots and our own unconscious biases. It also is the beginning of making and measuring progress. As Max de Pree said in his book *Leadership Is an Art*, "The number one job of a leader is to define reality."[6]

EQUAL PAY FOR EQUAL WORK

- "Men were paid more because they had a family they were responsible for and the females on the staff weren't the 'sole breadwinners.'"
- "Women, for years, were being paid much less than the men on staff who had less experience, less responsibility, and less education. So much depends on the lead pastor and his bias on the matter."
- "I was given a job after a male counterpart was promoted from the position, and when I took on the same role and the same job responsibilities, I was not given the same title nor the increase in compensation that was with my male predecessor's job. While I was grateful for the position and also the opportunity to grow in my gifting, I also was frustrated to not receive the same title and compensation for the job at

hand. Also, when I later had to look for a new job outside the organization, my previous title and salary did not really recognize the experience that I had gained to potential employers. It forced me to compete in a different bracket in the job market that was not equal to my experience."

- "Several times I have been given supervisory roles or duties without the title or pay of a supervisor."
- "I am paid part-time to do a job that two men do full-time at a different campus. As a woman, I am not expected to want compensation for my work—I am expected to be happy to serve."
- "Pay is very rarely equal. I know there are males on staff who do comparable or less than I do who make more money than me. Unfortunately, in the church world this is a delicate topic. No one goes into ministry for the money, nor do I ever want that to be an issue. I choose to trust God that all things will work out in the end. However, with full transparency, the double pay standard does frustrate me at times."[7]

These are just a few of the hundreds of comments and stories of women who receive less pay and benefits than men on the team who do similar work and carry similar responsibilities—in many cases, it was the exact same job description.

In America, women earn approximately 80 cents for every dollar a man earns for the same work. That 20 percent gap adds up to more than $10,000 per year in median earnings. This means the average female will lose $418,000 over a forty-year career compared with her male counterparts, and the gap is often larger among higher-paying jobs.

This disparity often grows even bigger because added benefits, such as raises and retirement contributions, are often based on a percentage of salary. A small discrepancy early in one's career can be really significant over a lifetime. It is estimated that the average female will have to stay in the workforce an additional ten years longer than a man in order to earn the same amount. And this is not even considering any time off or limiting career choices made to prioritize maternity leave or raising children.

Hispanic women earn even less: only 54 cents to every dollar. This means a Latina will lose out on more than $1 million over her career for doing the same work, simply because of her gender and ethnic minority status.[8]

We are not talking about administrative, supportive, or clerical roles versus educated, professional, or leadership roles. This is the pay discrepancy for the *same work*. I was surprised to learn that in secretarial roles, which are female dominated, men earn an average of 14 percent more than women.[9]

Even in churches where there are strong role differences based on gender, most people would agree that if a man and a woman are performing the same job, they should receive the same pay and benefits. In church work, however, this can sometimes get overlooked, dismissed, or even be an unintended "leftover" from hiring practices from a previous era. According to one study, even when presented with clear data of inequitable pay for equal work, only 61 percent of white men acknowledged this was unfair.[10] In another study focused on church leadership, female pastors who are married and mothers earned significantly less than their male counterparts in the same role: only 72 cents on the dollar.[11] The assumption is these women are not able to perform as well because of their responsibilities at home, even though the men are also married and have children. Sometimes our unconscious biases can create rationales to justify all sorts of decisions.

One of the most frequent justifications I have heard as to why churches pay men more than women is because they have families to support (i.e., they are the "breadwinner"). I've even seen men with more children be paid more simply because of the sizes of their families, not because they have more responsibilities or perform better.

Although this can seem generous and helpful in the moment, in the long term it can really limit your church's ability to hire and fire based on performance, and limits your ability to reward people in fair and equitable ways. And it begs the question: When someone's wife starts working or their children leave home, does their salary go back down? Usually not. It is also unfair to single people, who are often asked to work more or accept less pay because "they don't have a family to go home to." These kinds of clear inconsistencies usually end up eroding trust and diminishing team productivity, especially if there is not an opportunity to openly discuss the issues.

There are also unintended consequences of male-dominated structures, and this shows up a lot through intangible benefits. Loving and thankful church members are amazing at generously giving not only to their organized church but also directly to pastors and their families. Just in my small world I'm aware of my male colleagues receiving fully paid family vacations, ongoing lawn care, out-of-state marriage retreats, father-son outdoor adventure experiences, weekly childcare, meals, cars, hardwood flooring throughout their homes, kitchen makeovers, professional and personal clothing, designer shoes, books, and paid college tuition. I've also experienced male pastors participating on mission trips or being with their kids during church camps without having to pay or take vacation days, while women were required to do both.

Let me be clear that I am thrilled that the men and their families were blessed in these many ways. When you carry the burden of people's needs day in and day out, these types of rewards go a long way in encouraging a leader and his family. But the unintended consequence is that these "extras" are rarely extended to a female leader or her family. The result is that women on the ministry team not only receive less income and benefits, but they also have far fewer, if any, ministry perks and are missing out on one of the many blessings of serving and leading in a faith community.

While church leadership cannot directly influence the choices of congregants who show preference to male staff members, they need to be aware of how these inconsistencies affect female leaders and consider how they might be able to model equitable support and appreciation, as well as use their influence to make sure everyone on their staff is recognized and appreciated by their church family.

We've mentioned previously the tax benefits that employees who are "licensed for ministry" receive. In the past, I've seen men in clearly non-pastoral roles have access to this benefit simply because they are men who work at a church. A facilities manager usually does not meet the qualifications for a license to minister, yet this benefit is often used to increase a male employee's recruitment package, especially if he is coming from the marketplace. At the same time, many women in ministry roles do meet the qualifications and yet do not receive the licensed endorsement or the tax benefit. Cleaning up this inconsistency will go a long way in restoring trust with your team and integrity in your organizational systems and the government. Plus your female leaders will receive a deserved financial bump that doesn't cost the church anything.

Recently, I have begun seeing several churches taking strides in equitability by offering licensed status to women even without the official title of "pastor" or weekend teaching responsibilities, as many female ministry leaders clearly meet the qualifications.

ACCURATE TITLES

Another popular topic in our interviews and survey was the job titles given to male versus female staff. Of our survey participants, 42 percent had been given titles that either didn't match their male counterparts, or didn't accurately describe what they were responsible for doing.[12]

Almost everyone commented that, to them personally, titles were not their main priority. But when it comes to leading effectively, titles carry influence and communicate one's role on the team and within the organization. These are critical factors in leading successfully, especially with volunteers who aren't in the office every day. When asked how important it is to have accurate titles for female leaders in churches, more than one thousand survey participants rated it an 83 out of 100.[13]

Several women were given two titles—one to use within the church that wouldn't raise any concerns and one to use outside the church to better describe their role. I know I have personally had a handful of ambiguous and somewhat mystifying titles on my business cards that I've come to affectionately call "girl titles." You can usually tell the job is important, but there's no way to figure out why.

The most common difference is in the use of the title "pastor." As you can guess, this is often connected to different theological viewpoints. Many churches have not yet clearly defined their position on women in leadership, however, so the different titles are confusing and are often interpreted as devaluing women. Many churches have adopted a practice of calling male leaders "pastors" and female leaders "directors." In most cases, the two roles function basically the same, although pastors may be called on for certain roles of spiritual authority that directors are not. Performing weddings and funerals, handling pastoral on-call duties, and preaching or teaching God's Word in formal worship services are examples of activities often reserved for those with the title of pastor.

Other churches have decided to call all their organizational leaders (male and female) "directors" while reserving the title of pastor for those who have completed seminary and ordination. This gives the added benefit of allowing people to take on the organizational leadership role while growing into the spiritual authority role, if they choose. It also helps communicate that pastoring is more than "being a man on staff" and is instead about training, affirmed calling, giftedness, and fruitfulness. After all, there are many men in churches and on church staffs who are not qualified to be pastors.

On the other hand, there are hundreds of examples of women who are essentially leading teams, projects, and in some cases, entire ministry departments, but were given titles that do not match the level of authority or responsibility they carry. Coordinator, assistant, on the executive team, special assistant, champion, specialist, and developer are various titles given to women leaders. Although these are mostly reasonable titles, they don't articulate their level of leadership or the authority they have to make decisions. Of course, every person on staff is under someone else's authority, but women often do double duty—they need to lead well but also overly communicate someone else's decision or preference, even if that has been fully delegated to them.

For example, let's pretend that Kayla is responsible for all weekend welcome teams at her large campus. She oversees the logistics for all weekend services and special events, including the five volunteer teams made up of more than one hundred greeters and ushers and communion, parking lot, and information table volunteers. If Kayla's title is "assistant," those one hundred volunteers will likely answer her emails and come to her if they want to make an appointment with the pastor she works for. If her title is "coordinator," most of those one hundred people would come to her with questions about their volunteer schedule or if they needed a new name tag. But if Kayla's title is "director" or "manager," those volunteers know that they can also go to her for a problem they are facing on the team, with an idea about how to improve the flow of people after services, and to make an introduction of a newly recruited volunteer. And if her title is "pastor," then they also know they can go to her for spiritual guidance and prayer, to get help with a problem in their family that the church might have a resource for, and to update her on how the small group they tried last week turned out.

By giving all leaders, male and female, titles that communicate your expectations and what they have to offer those they lead, you not only make them more effective in their ministry, but you take a load off the rest of the pastoral team because, as we all know, those one hundred volunteers will end up talking to someone!

One survey participant shared her story:

I was hired in as a coordinator, even though I had an MA from a seminary and had taught grad students for two years. The majority of my male co-workers were hired in as pastors, even though most of them had not attended seminary. When I attempted to be promoted to a director-level position (the only option available to women), I was denied. It was frustrating. I found it hard to live off of what I was paid, and the assumption was that if you were a woman, you either lived with your parents or were married. I was neither. I often was referred to as an admin or my boss's assistant, even though I created content and taught at retreats. Working there felt like a constant battle, and very few people were willing to have an open conversation about the environment for women.[14]

Another said:

When I was hired at my church I was "hourly," which was kind of great because I worked tons of hours, but it made me feel like it was just a job. My role was with student ministries, and I was doing much more than administrative stuff—even writing sermons to be delivered by the youth pastor, and even once delivered by yours truly. I was counseling the female students and running youth events entirely on my own. I had a degree and already had a few years of experience working professionally with teens. Eventually my designation was changed to a salaried employee and remained that way. This small change, for some reason, made a world of difference in how I viewed my position at the church. It truly added value and professionalized my job description.[15]

BENEFITS THAT BENEFIT WOMEN

As companies and churches have become more serious about engaging gender equality and communicating to women that they want them not only to join the team but to stay on the team, they've discovered some creative benefits that support women in the seasons of life that are unique to them.

FAMILY BENEFITS

Having children is one of the most challenging seasons for a female leader. Not only is there the whole baby world to figure out, but trying to decide what this means for ministry, long-term leadership, and career building can be confusing and overwhelming.

- Do I keep working?
- Do I stay home?
- Is there an option for part-time?
- Will I be able to come back and lead?
- Can I even afford to not work?

Offering paid or affordable benefits for maternity leave and offering creative working arrangements, especially during early childhood years and summers, can give the female leaders on your team a pathway for winning both at home and at church. In fact, 54 percent of our survey participants believe that working at a church helps female leaders who are also mothers. This is vastly different from the marketplace, where challenges and biases against being a mom are common enough to have their own term, the "Motherhood Penalty."[16]

Personally, I think churches are in a wonderful position to be able to competitively offer creative, family-friendly, professional leadership roles for women since family life and parenting well are foundational to our belief system and values. Wouldn't it be great if churches could lead the way in this?

Since many women who work at churches are part-time, family benefits are important to look at regardless of full-time status. Part-time work is also a wonderful way to keep a female leader engaged and connected with the team and continuing to learn and contribute to her ministry while her kids are young. Within a few years, she will be able to step back into higher levels of leadership faster and hit the ground running. This can be a game changer in developing your leadership bench in the long term.

One survey participant explained her struggle with working and raising a family:

> I only pastor part time. This is first due to funding of the church. But second, I am a mom and that does come first. As a female, you do have to be okay with the fact that women go through more seasons. There's a part of me that hates it because I do want more ministry opportunities, but my family comes first. They won't be in my home forever, and I need to trust God that *He* is the one who will accelerate me and open doors for me when my time becomes more open.[17]

In addition, allowing sick time to be used for ill family members and children can go a long way in allowing women to care for their families during tough times. Offering benefits such as FMLA

(Family and Medical Leave Act), short-term disability, life insurance, and other supplemental insurances, even if your staff is too small to be required to do so, allows for families to be taken care of if an employee becomes sick or injured, or even during happy events, like childbirth. Since most Americans live paycheck to paycheck, these benefits are incredibly attractive to female leaders and offer a peace of mind while working.

Other ideas that significantly benefit women include offering childcare on-site or close by, negotiating lowered tuition to private Christian schools, allowing "work from home" days, giving one weekend off a month to come to church as a family, providing lactation rooms, allocating funds for counseling services for them or their families, and offering adoption benefits.

FLEXIBLE SCHEDULES

Motherhood is a long-term responsibility that doesn't end when kids start school. Parenting through all ages and stages requires energy, engagement, and flexibility. But so do the other seasons of a woman's life, such as caring for aging parents, being a grandparent, menopause, and even being single. Although it's easy to assume single people have more time, they often have a greater need for flexibility in order to visit with or stay connected to family, build their social support systems, and take advantage of opportunities unique to their season of life.

Most of the marketplace workforce has switched to a more fluid and flexible work schedule, mostly made possible by advancements in technology that allow one to work from virtually anywhere at any time. Offering flexibility for both men and women helps support your female leaders and develops a culture of delivering results over the number of hours in the office. For parents, this allows them to do things like drop off or pick up their kids from school, attend a concert in the midmorning, stay home with a sick child, or connect with the other moms at a classmate's birthday party, while still delivering on their jobs well.

For leaders in other seasons of life, this might mean being able to take their aging parent or grandparent to the doctor, work on a home renovation project, travel, go back to school, work through a health care crisis, or even start a side hustle. Most leaders thrive in this kind of autonomy and flexibility, often accomplishing even more than they would with strict work hours and a defined location.[18]

Jerry Hurley from Life.Church described it like this:

On one hand, you could say, "Well, you don't have to treat a working mom any different than anybody else." I understand that, and I agree with that. However, if you're a working mom, you know that there's a lot of things that you have to do that the average male worker doesn't have to do. We can say it shouldn't be different or it's not different, but the reality is, if you're smart, you're going to recognize that actually there is a difference.

One of the ways that we make benefits available to all people is by providing our team with an unlimited leave policy. We encourage our team to take the time they need when they need it. This enables us to create very flexible schedules and a very flexible work environment that is helpful for every team member, male or female, but it is particularly beneficial for working moms. Culturally, too, everyone needs to know that using that benefit is acceptable.

We work very hard to make sure that we don't just say that balancing life and family are very important to us, but we create the culture for it.[19]

In addition, many people are figuring out ways to work less, even if that means earning less money. Working half to two-thirds of a full-time job has allowed them to still be engaged at work without losing out on their other priorities. Job sharing, contract work, and "out of the box" job opportunities are great ways for women to be able to maximize their contribution in ministry and still fully meet the other callings in their life. For example, I know several women who work very intense schedules during the school year, but then very few hours during the summer, when their ministry is slower and their kids are home on vacation. There are often a couple of tough weeks of overlap, but it is worth it for the connection they can maintain the rest of the year.

EDUCATION AND DEVELOPMENT OPPORTUNITIES

Although this is not a benefit unique for women, women do tend to have less education, resources, and opportunities for development than men, both formally and informally. Set aside extra money in your church's budget to develop female leaders, including paying for and giving time off to attend conferences, workshops, and even gain additional degrees; these are incredibly attractive incentives to female leaders and show your commitment to their development and long-term contribution. It is also important to explain these benefits to women and regularly encourage them to take advantage of them.

I remember being on a church staff in my late twenties and realizing too late that the church offered low-cost seminary classes on-site to our ministry staff. I'm confident I would have been allowed to take advantage of this alongside all the men, but I didn't know it existed, and no one thought to offer it to me.

WORK-LIFE BALANCE

Having a healthy soul and being a good example of how to live in today's busy culture is important for everyone in ministry, both men and women. Raising the bar on this conversation helps communicate to the female leaders on your team that you not only want the church to win but you want them, and their families, to win as well. Regularly teach your staff about the importance of soul care as well as practical advice on how to prioritize it with the demands of ministry. Offer days off during the year to be dedicated to personal, spiritual growth. Offer books, resources, and studies for leaders to be able to grow on their own and in community with other ministry leaders. And, most important, be sure to model a healthy and God-honoring work-life balance in your own personal life, ministry, and leadership role.

HONEST PERFORMANCE REVIEWS

As I talk with church leaders, especially male leaders, one of the biggest challenges of getting women at their leadership tables and into their development pipelines is dealing with women who want to be there but aren't good at leading. They often don't have the skills or the gifting required to lead. But how do you say that to someone? How can you champion women and still say no to those women who should be serving in other ways?

In my experience, one of the critical elements missing for most women, especially women on church staffs or in women-based ministries, is honest and constructive feedback. I've heard it said that churches can become sick from a "case of niceness," where honesty and candor are commonly overridden by insincere kindness and flattery. This can be detrimental to the development of female leaders who are capable, resilient, and confident.

One of my interviewees described the best-case scenario for her as a young, female leader as "tough jobs with great bosses."[20] Unfortunately, most women don't receive the kind of honest, real-time feedback needed to become self-aware and grow as a leader. Even if they are given opportunities, they don't learn the same lessons or grow in the same ways men do who receive more descriptive and straightforward feedback.

In a recent research study, women were discovered to be much less likely to receive specific feedback tied to their performance outcomes, regardless of whether it was positive or constructive.[21] In other words, even when they did well, they didn't know exactly why. And if they did poorly, they weren't sure why and what to do to be better the next time. In fact, vague praise such as, "You did a really good job," is given more frequently to women. Men, on the other hand, tend to receive much more instructive feedback, such as, "You need to work on _____ skill. Once you learn that, I'd like to involve you in _____." Without this type of detail or next steps, it is difficult for any leader to develop.

The tendency to give women shallow feedback with few steps for improvement creates this "case of niceness." I've met women who have spent years serving on church teams but never made it out of the secretarial pool, and sometimes with understandable reasons. In an effort to value these women and appreciate them, many of their leaders shower them with vague praise, introduce them publicly as the "glue" who "really holds the place together," and celebrate their value on the team frequently.

To be fair, there are many wonderful and capable women who really are the glue that holds a team together. But unfortunately, many times that is not the case, and these leaders are not being fully honest. Sometimes these women are still in their same position because they have terrible attitudes. I have witnessed some shocking behaviors when their leaders leave the room. I've met very few who have ever recruited or equipped a volunteer. Many of them constantly complain about all they do and claim that they are not valued, and think that if someone would just listen to their ideas, everything would run so much better.

Well, guess what? Attitude, equipping others, and problem-solving are all key components of effective leadership. Yet these women have no idea about that. They've been allowed to be discontent, negative, and undeveloped. Unfortunately, they have a long way to go, even if they do have gifts that can be used in a leadership role.

As you begin to develop female leaders, be sure to give honest feedback to those who want to lead but aren't ready yet. It's tough. It's awkward. It will be painful for them, and probably for you as well. This is why 360-degree feedback can be so helpful. Many of us don't know how to give good feedback. It's hard to be clear and objective. But getting input from an employee's leaders, peers, and direct reports provides enough perspectives and insights to give detailed feedback with intentional steps for development.

Then, as you continue to work with her, be sure to give her frequent and real-time feedback on those developmental milestones. Most organizations have moved away from formal feedback once a year to more frequent feedback. This has been shown to be especially helpful for women.[22] You may have leadership there that you didn't know was lying dormant. Perhaps her first step is to learn how to recruit and develop a team. Who couldn't use a handful of new office volunteers running errands and providing administrative support? Or you both might discover new gifts and abilities that free her to fully contribute to her current job, without a desire to advance any higher. Either way, moving toward more honest and intentional feedback will allow the right conversations to happen with the right female leaders and take the pressure off the unspoken idea that inviting women into leadership means that you have to allow *all* women to lead.

METRICS FOR HIRING AND PROMOTIONS

There is lots of research and documentation about how women are not hired or promoted as often as men. The only real way to know if your church is making improvements in this area, however, is to start tracking your own data on recruitment, interviewing, hiring, and promotions. Since you can't change what you don't measure, you'll need to establish a baseline of metrics that you will follow over the next few months and years.

Since the real value of measurements like this grows over time, spending the effort to decide what to measure and how to measure is worth it. For example, if in five years you want to see how women are progressing through your leadership-training programs, you will need to start asking about gender on the applications *now*. As a team, ask yourselves, "what you want to be different by this time next year? In the next ten years?" When you get clear on how you want things to look in the future, figuring out what to look at and start measuring today becomes a lot easier.

What to measure will depend on your organization, your church's long-term vision, and your theological position, but here are some suggestions to get your team to start thinking. They are positioned in order from the simplest to more detailed. I recommend doing at least the first five. The rest can be adjusted depending on the size of your church, volunteer base, and staff team.

Minimum Baseline Metrics

1. What is our gender ratio for paid staff leadership roles in our church or ministry? (It is best to take out administrative/clerical roles and focus on ministry/leadership roles.)
2. What is our gender ratio in volunteer leadership roles?
3. What is our gender ratio in volunteer roles?

Items 1–3 speak to the effectiveness of your leadership pipeline.

4. In our leadership training programs or classes, what percent are women and what percent are men? (This is a predictor of what your future ratios will look like. It could also indicate if you have strong female leaders reporting to undertrained male leaders.)
5. What is our gender ratio in our executive/senior leadership team and director/management team? (This addresses

having female perspective in high-level leadership decisions and what women may perceive as "possible" for them.)

Additional Metrics

6. Fill out gender percentage breakdowns at every level of your entire leadership pipeline.
7. Compare gender ratios by ministry.
8. Compare gender ratios in volunteer and leadership roles based on age and ministry. (Young adult and student ministries are excellent environments to raise up young ministry leaders. If you have good ratios here, you'll start to see them grow into ministry leaders throughout the church. If you don't, you'll know you need to investigate why.)
9. Compare employment ratios by gender. To do this, don't simply use titles. Categorize all employees by similar levels of responsibility (What type of responsibility and level of independence is exhibited?) and span of oversight (How many people, types of projects, or tasks?). Be sure to compare what employees are *actually* doing, not what is on their job descriptions or assumptions about what their jobs might entail. Once you have them in buckets, compare the following:

   a. Titles
   b. Pay—amount and exempt status. Be sure to include overtime hours and pay rates.
   c. Benefits
   d. Education level
   e. Licensure and/or ordination
   f. Educational benefits available (in-house trainings, books, conferences, college reimbursement)

g. Educational benefits accessed (Have they been formally invited to take advantage of their opportunities? And what is the percentage of men and women who are accessing these benefits?)

h. On-the-job leadership development opportunities (supervisor's skill level of developing team members, mentoring from higher level leader, shadowing leaders, "stretch" opportunities offered with feedback)

i. Opportunities for same-gender leader connections/coaching

j. Spouse/family connection and support

k. Number of years in the same level/title (even if in same role, there should be advancement as levels of expertise increase. For example, pastor level 1, 2, 3 or ministry assistant level 1, 2, 3)

l. Average length of time until promotion

m. Average raise year over year

As you calculate these metrics, consider pulling data about other minorities for whom you want to be more intentional. It's so much easier to do this all at one time. If you aren't sure what else you should be looking at, pull a simple demographic report of the three-mile radius of your church or campus location. Take the top three ethnic groups and see if your leadership is accurately reflecting the community you are called to reach. You can also add people with disabilities or within certain age ranges, or other minority groups that you feel are close to God's heart for your church.

10. Look at hiring ratios. While quota systems are often counterproductive, setting targets for female hires can produce measurable results.

      a. Gender ratios of applicants (speaks to recruiting strategies and overall church culture)

      b. Ratio of those who make it to an interview

      c. Ratio of those hired (could point to a bias in your hiring practices and decisions)

Chase Oaks Church in Dallas has been challenging its leaders to have more ethnic and gender diversity in their recruiting pools. In fact, the executive pastor recently decided not to consider any final employee candidates from his ministry leaders unless they had also interviewed a certain number of female candidates. It was challenging for the team to look in new networks and recruit in new ways, but they did it. They added three highly qualified female leaders to the interview mix and ended up giving one of them the job.[23]

11. Evaluate staff diversity trainings. Determine the percentage of staff and volunteer leaders who have refreshed their understanding of your beliefs, vision, and expectations when it comes to diversity issues. Even though diversity training has undergone scrutiny for not being very effective, it is still incredibly helpful when trying to introduce new thinking around the benefits of diversity on team performance and how bias plays a role in our everyday lives. It is also a great way to introduce common language among team members and normalize discussing such sensitive and sometimes highly charged issues.

12. Determine how employee benefits are being accessed. Are women knowledgeable and taking full advantage of the benefits you provide? These are offerings intended to communicate value and investment in your leaders who are continuing to lead even during different seasons of their life. Look at the following:

a. The number of women accessing full family leave benefits (A low number could indicate that they do not know fully what is available to them, that they don't believe it is offered to all staff members, or that they fear using the benefits because of negative consequences to their standing at work.)
b. The percentage of females investing in your retirement plan
c. The average number of days female employees take for maternity leave (The higher the number, the more confident they are of their ability to continue in their career during motherhood years.)

As you begin to collect data, you'll likely start to see some trends. For example, perhaps you don't have any women applying for ministry job openings. This could point to an awareness issue within your church that these are roles open for females. Or perhaps the way the job description is written is communicating something unintended, or the places it is being advertised don't have many female leaders. There are many articles online and resources available within the HR community to help overcome these types of barriers for developing female leaders within all levels of leadership.

PASTORS' WIVES

Some of the comments from our survey participants had to do not only with being a female leader but also with being married to a pastor. There are many pastors' wives who enjoy being in a supportive and background role, but there are also strong female leaders who are married to pastors yet are looking for their own opportunities to lead.

Unfortunately, this gets complicated.

On one hand, there is leadership to be found *alongside* one's husband. This tends to be an extension of his leadership and employment. In many church cultures there are strong expectations, either overt or subtle, that the pastor's wife should be serving essentially full-time in ministry with her husband for no pay or actual authority of her own. One woman shared, "For years I was unpaid because they paid my husband, so it was like a 'two for one' special. But after ten years and my husband, our executive pastor, and the district overseer going to bat for me with church council, they put me on paid staff. I have paved the way for this to never happen again on my watch."[24]

Depending on the couple, working together can be beautiful as they complement each other's skills and seamlessly lead their family and the church together. Many church plants, student ministries, and missionary endeavors are accomplished primarily through this marriage partnership. From the people I've talked to, this works best in smaller church or ministry environments where there is high relational leadership and the ability for everyone to be easily interconnected and on the same page.

One pastor's wife discussed her experience:

> I've never been treated as "less than." As a matter of fact, I currently have the problem of folks trying to assign me the role of co-pastor with my husband. I am not a pastor, I am not called to pastor, and I always gently explain that is not my role. This is a new experience in our current ministry setting. I love serving alongside my husband, but I've never had any desire to be his equal in the area of leadership.[25]

This "shared leadership" can be harder in larger team environments, where it is more challenging to understand who actually works for the church, what their roles are, and to whom to go for which concern.

I was recently coaching a female leader who works for a pastor who co-leads with his wife in a large, matrix church leadership structure. The lines between their roles are foggy and have fallen into how they function within their marriage and family responsibilities. The wife, who doesn't work full-time nor is able to attend all staff meetings, gets all the emails for both of them, is the main communication hub for the team, and directs most of the logistics. The husband/pastor is distant, allows his wife to be the "relational one," and only addresses the team when something goes wrong. This situation is very confusing for the team and has left my coaching client trying to respect and honor both leaders, but not having the clarity, direction, feedback, or relational equity needed to succeed in her job.

For pastors' wives, this can also be confusing.

- "Should I step in and lead?"
- "Where are my boundaries?"
- "Am I part of the leadership team or not?"
- "Where, exactly, do I fit in?"

One survey participant commented:

I am both the lead pastor's wife and a credentialed minister leading two areas of ministry, but I am not on the payroll. While at an event venue with the entire staff to scope it out as an option for an upcoming event, the executive pastor introduced everyone with the title "pastor (name)" except me. I was the pastor's wife. Now, I am not ashamed of that title, but in that situation it painted me as a meddling wife and not part of the pastoral team.[26]

Clearly defining roles for all leaders, regardless of whom they are married to, is critical in helping develop female leaders. Just as it is damaging to give female leaders on the team responsibilities without the authority required to do the job, it is also damaging to give some women authority without any real responsibility or accountability because of whom they are married to, related to, dating, or close friends with. This type of nepotism is dangerous for any family member or preferred relationship.

This can also include other leadership roles such as elders, deacons, and denominational leaders, or any other role of influence in your church. Leadership is a healthy and balanced combination of both responsibility *and* authority. The more aligned these are, the more effective and healthy your teams will be.

On the other hand is an expectation that a pastor's wife is just that: her husband's wife, without any gifts, abilities, and passions unique to her. As one woman commented, "Despite my years of experience, education, and denominational credentials, when my husband and I were called to be campus pastors at a new church, the senior pastor told me, 'You'll just morph into whatever your husband is doing.'"[27]

Giving all women, including pastors' wives or the wives of other leaders, opportunities to identify and explore their gifts and discover the unique call God has on their lives is incredibly important when working to develop female leaders throughout your church. It is rarely helpful to assume that simply because a woman is married to a church leader, she also is a mature, qualified, and competent leader. Every woman deserves the opportunity to learn, grow, and be affirmed in her gifts and abilities on her own merit.

A pastor's wife explained:

I think for me, I've always just been the "pastor's wife" to people. "Oh, what a nice support for her husband." I am his biggest fan and supporter, but for a long time I think that has clouded my mentality of what I am capable of or what God has for me. Until the last five or six years, I've probably had a "side-lined" mentality and haven't stepped up or pushed myself to be anything other than "the pastor's wife" (although I have done a lot in ministry). I am in a new season where God has awakened something in me. He has more of a purpose for me than to be sidelined. He has given me a voice and a platform and He wants to use me. . . . I just need to say yes. So finally, a year ago, I started taking university classes that I've thought about and looked into doing multiple times over the last sixteen years. I now have one more class for certification and then I will start working on my license level. And it isn't that I "need" those to be used by God, obviously, but I am pushing myself to learn and grow as a person and a leader. I also have purposed to be available and if I feel led by the Holy Spirit to give a message, to share a word, to pray for people, etc., I'm just going to step out and do it.[28]

Unfortunately, whether we want to admit it or not, we all carry some sort of unconscious bias that affects the leadership decisions we make and, ultimately, the people on the receiving end of our bias. Taking a close look at our human resource practices, discussing these sensitive issues in an open and collaborative way, and holding ourselves accountable through metrics can ensure that we are truly leading in a way that aligns with our beliefs and values. As one woman from our survey said:

Let's not do women any extra favors, or promote them, just because of gender. This defeats the purpose of demonstrating equal capability and, I believe, decreases the validity of women in leadership roles in some people's thinking. If I'm only at the table because someone needs to fill a female "quota," I'd rather find another table to sit at. However, let us ensure we are watching for and providing opportunities for women to grow, lead, and advance in our churches and organizations. And let us look for ways to provide positive female leadership examples for our emerging female (and male) leaders. I am thankful for the contexts in which I've served where I have been encouraged, been given equal opportunity, and have been challenged to go "first" as a woman in leadership.[29]

Best Practice #8

TAKE ON YOUR CULTURE

I couldn't believe it."

The executive pastor had finished his story and looked at me questioningly. He had been so excited to offer two female leaders on their children's ministry team a promotion. Their church had been working to raise the awareness of women leaders and realized a big part of that was giving them the titles, pay, and benefits that matched their level of leadership and pastoral care of people. He couldn't wait to meet with each one, celebrate their individual contributions, explain how each promotion was well deserved, and congratulate them on becoming pastors.

He got turned down point-blank by both of them. And he had no idea why.

I explained that he is working against a strong and influential culture. Not every woman is going to jump at the chance to be promoted or take on a leadership opportunity, especially if it feels like a surprise. I explained that for many women, being asked out of the blue to be a ministry leader or pastor would be like someone walking into his office and saying, "Congratulations! We've decided you would make a great astronaut. NASA wants you to fly up in space by yourself next week in an experimental rocket. We know this has never been done before and many people disagree with us trying out this idea, but we think you'll do great. Aren't you so happy?"

While NASA might think this sounds like a great honor and obviously a unique opportunity, you would probably be thinking about the fact that you know nothing about being an astronaut. You've never thought of going into space before. It's never even been an idea in your head. In fact, someone has probably told you other things are far more likely than you flying to the moon. It doesn't matter if he assures you that your abilities are more than adequate for this mission. In fact, the job you have been doing the last few years has been perfect training for this opportunity. You are more than qualified, even though you have no NASA education, no training, no astronaut experience, and the only thing going through your mind are scenes from the movies about astronauts who are usually trying to overcome some sort of life-threatening space crisis. Although you would appreciate being asked, your reply would likely be, "No, thank you."

This is what it can feel like to a woman who has new opportunities suddenly thrust upon her. It goes against much of what she has been taught, and in many cases, the thought has honestly never entered her head as an option, or if it has, she has surrendered any sort of hope for it. For a man who has been watching pastoral "astronauts" his whole life, he likely imagines what it would be like to have that job. He has friends who are astronauts. He's probably even done some low-level "astronaut-type" activities as a volunteer, while a woman may never have even thought of it.

In addition, there is a thick culture in every church that many women, especially those who are going "first," will bump up against. It can be challenging, hurtful, confusing, and in some cases quite painful.

I remember talking with a newly hired female executive director who had recently met with the usher team for the first time. They had not received much attention in the past, and her job was to help resource them and serve as a liaison for whatever they needed from the staff. The usher leaders spent the first half of the meeting explaining in no uncertain terms that they did not believe in women teaching men. Despite her years of professional experience and organizational access, she simply replied, "Okay. I will do my very best to make sure you don't learn anything from me."

Even though theologically she was not stepping on any boundaries by helping them get new offering baskets or ordering replacement usher shirts, the underlying culture was going to prevent her from being able to help that team. Everyone loses when our culture isn't ready or willing to embrace new ideas.

Peter Drucker said it best: "Culture eats strategy for breakfast."[1] The cultures of our churches, leadership teams, and organizations are the unique interpersonal environments in which we lead, work, and worship. They are sometimes hard to describe because they are often "caught" rather than "taught," and are based on a combination of underlying beliefs, assumptions, values, and ways of interacting with one another. But they are powerful. The best ideas in the world cannot overpower culture, even if people really want to see change. You have to get in and shift the culture before your plans and strategies can actually take root and produce the fruit you are looking to harvest.

I like to think about organizational cultures as ecosystems. They are environments that both influence, and are influenced by, those who live there. A deep, thick forest, for example, is a community of a variety of plants, animals, and organisms that are very different yet beautifully interdependent. If something is missing, the whole system gets impacted. Ecosystems are complex and interconnected and not easy to change; yet, at the same time, they can be altered. They are alive and organic and constantly adjusting themselves to keep everything alive and fruitful.

The same is true in our churches. We are a community of lots of different thoughts and ideas who influence one another deeply. What happens in one part of the body impacts everyone. We are complex and interconnected and not easy to change. We are alive and organic and constantly adjusting (hopefully) to keep ourselves fruitful. In fact, we often have several ecosystems, or subcultures, that live together and make up who we are as a church body.

But an incredible thing happens when two ecosystems transition into each other, like a mountain forest transitioning into a desert. Or where the mouth of a river carrying fresh water opens up into an ocean of strong seawater. The two ecosystems overlap and influence each other, creating a third environment where the plants and wildlife have an abundance of diversity and richness that neither ecosystem could have on its own.

In Florida, we call these mixed fresh and saltwater areas "brackish water." It's not totally fresh water and yet it isn't seawater; it's in between. The same goes for the soil, vegetation, animal life, and insects; it's a blend of the two. Often, unique plants or wildlife can only exist in the biodiversity of these two interconnected environments. This integrated space is called an ecotone. "Eco" from the word *ecology*, and "tone" from the Greek word *tonos*, meaning tension.[2] In other words, an ecotone is a place where two strong ecosystems connect and out of the tension comes something even more abundant, rich, prolific, and beautiful.[3]

When we lead change within our cultures, we lead the tension of two ecosystems colliding. One established set of ideas, values, and behaviors begins to influence and change another set of ideas, values, and behaviors. If we don't lead it well, it can be a blunt, harsh collision in which both sides are damaged and stay disconnected. But if we do the hard work to intentionally develop connection and acceptance, we can harness the tension and create an abundant, rich, and beautiful environment that is even more fruitful and prolific than either culture could be on its own.

But it's not easy.

Unique cultures are defined by their language, boundaries, and symbols.[4] These are the raw ingredients of every organizational ecosystem, and they can be incredibly helpful and positive. When something doesn't line up with the culture, it is easy to see and address. Even when left on its own, the culture will automatically reproduce itself for better or worse. Healthy environments, where all three of these components are aligned in the right direction, keep everyone moving together. Like a crew team when all the oars are rowing in the same direction and at the same time, these strong cultures are powerful, even unstoppable.

To shift culture, then, requires taking on each of these three aspects.[5] You have to mix up the ingredients of the ecosystem to get a different environment and therefore different fruit. The organizations that have made the most progress in helping female leaders develop and contribute to their church bodies have strategically and methodically taken on their culture. It's not easy and it's not fast, but it is necessary for real change.

LANGUAGE AND VOCABULARY

Words matter. Language creates mind-set. Stories communicate culture. What we say and how we say it makes a difference.

This shows up frequently in how we set up leaders to lead. A strong introduction is a powerful tool to pave the way for someone to lead a meeting, an initiative, a message, a ministry, or a department.[6] Introductions for male leaders often set them up to have influence, as they are often automatically introduced with information about their accomplishments, past performance, tangible results, and drive. Women leaders, on the other hand, are more commonly introduced by their personality, their relationships (whom they are married to or friends with), their outward appearance, and their teamwork abilities. Both are true, but unfortunately, this unintentionally sets a woman up to have to prove her ability and competency before she can actually begin leading. Choosing our words carefully and focusing on a female leader's accomplishments, independence, and initiative will set her up to lead well from the start.

This can also show up in how we communicate about the importance of a woman's voice, especially in official settings such as events and worship services. When I was a teenager, I remember listening to a Christian radio station broadcasting an annual conference for pastors. Every preacher was insightful, inspiring, and spiritually challenging. I realize now that they were also all men except for one. Joni Erickson Tada was a "guest speaker" who "shared."

Now, I'm pretty sure that they were all "guest speakers," since it was a conference, but she was the only one introduced this way. She spoke the same amount of time and on the same stage as everyone else. She taught from God's Word. She used personal stories to drive home her points and leveraged the platform to bring awareness to her nonprofit organization. The only differences were that she was a quadriplegic and a woman—and she got a standing ovation at the end. Yet her introduction and the description of what she was doing were totally different from the men's.

Taking a close look at how you use language is very helpful. You can evaluate any words that your culture might be specifically using for certain genders even though the words don't necessarily have a gender connection. Such as preaching versus teaching or sharing.

Leading versus facilitating. Or holding accountable versus influencing. Even changing our common vernacular from "the guys" to "the team" sends a message. None of the high-level female leaders I interviewed ever expressed being offended by being "one of the guys" or being called something more masculine (and everyone had been), but using inclusive language does communicate a value to those outside your team, especially young leaders who are watching and listening for what is possible for them. One female leader shared this story:

> We were announcing our newest campus pastors and we (staff ministry leaders) were all called forward to pray for them. The senior pastor said, "What a great team of guys this is," and the whole room burst out laughing because I'm standing there in the middle of the circle. It was a funny moment, but made me more painfully aware of what our bias is here. And I say all that with great love, but it's the truth. Another (male) leader texted me right away, "I am so thankful you are in your role and giving the young ladies on our team a vision of what can be."[7]

By the way, the reverse is true for female-dominated ministries, like children's ministry. Referring to the team as "the girls" or planning team activities that are usually enjoyed only by females is just as exclusionary.

When it comes to the language we use in our culture, it is not only what we say but what we don't say that is important. Generally speaking, our broader society tends to dismiss women and their perspectives. This is often done very subtly and can make it difficult for a woman to put her finger on what, exactly, just happened. But somehow she was not able to fully express her thought, and many times the discussion turns in such a way that someone else is given credit for her idea. She is left feeling cut off, interrupted, or ignored.

According to a *New York Times* article, "Researchers consistently

DEVELOPING FEMALE LEADERS

find that women are interrupted more and that men dominate conversations and decision-making, in corporate offices, town meetings,
school boards and the United States Senate."[8] The slang for this is *manterrupting*, and it is so common most people don't even notice that it
has happened.[9] As a team, it is critical to talk about what this looks
like, what leads to this (often urgency or highly charged topics), and
how you can help hold one another accountable. It might not even be
strictly a gender-based issue; oftentimes introverts' perspectives are
easily interrupted and overlooked in leadership conversations as well.

The goal is for everyone on your leadership team to have the ability to fully voice their perspectives, and that those perspectives are
each listened to and considered by the rest of the team. Collaboration
is not the same as consensus, but not listening fully to every person robs your team and your church from seeing as many sides of
the issue as possible before making a decision. As H. L. Mencken
reminded us: "For every complex problem there is a solution that is
neat, plausible, and wrong."[10]

BOUNDARIES AND BORDERS

For nations, borders are hard lines that are clearly marked and often
guarded. They show up on maps. Sometimes they are created or
reinforced by immovable landmarks, such as an ocean or a mountain
range. They tell you where this country begins and where it ends.

For teams and organizations, boundaries are more behavioral.
What kind of behaviors do we allow? What will we not tolerate?
What happens if someone violates a cultural boundary? How do
we celebrate and reinforce people who uphold our culture? Cultural
boundaries can feel a little less concrete, but they should still be
established, mapped out, and guarded. It's what creates your culture
and defines where it starts and where it ends.

Many teams have core values—those fundamental beliefs and guiding principles for a church or organization. But I've come to know several churches that also establish leadership values—those beliefs and guiding principles for the leaders of their organization. Leadership is a privilege and requires a higher level of commitment and often sacrifice. Especially in a church setting, separating out the attitudes, behaviors, and practices of leaders can be a very helpful tool in leading cultural change.

For example, it is not uncommon for someone to start attending church who has very little understanding of your beliefs or church culture. This person may say or do things in a way that is not in line with what most of the people in your church say or do. As a church, we want everyone to feel welcome. We are all equal at the foot of the cross, and this is an important part of ministering to a local community: come as you are and you will be loved and accepted. It is what God does for each of us.

However, He usually doesn't let us stay that way. Lifestyle choices and habits that are harmful to ourselves or others change over time as we grow in our relationship with the Lord and within a healthy community. As a leader, there are even some choices that aren't allowed, either biblically or because of a church's preferences. Outlining these "higher-level" behaviors and attitudes can help raise the bar on your culture and get everyone rowing in that new direction.

In Best Practice #2, we talked about the need to clearly define what you believe. These boundaries allow women within your culture to thrive as leaders without stopping short because of wrong assumptions. When it comes to nurturing the culture, however, it's critical to articulate both sides of that boundary. There may be some roles or responsibilities that women cannot have, but be sure to also communicate all the roles and responsibilities they can have. And both women and men need to know what these are because it's how the individual parts of your ecosystem work together and support one another.

One leader told me about a church that was having all sorts of bookkeeping and financial issues. Attending the church was a well-respected female CPA, but the elders refused to let her help them because she was a woman. She was more than capable of helping, as she had all sorts of expertise and an office full of quality employees who could have solved their problems for free, but they would not allow her to help because in their minds, they assumed that because a woman couldn't be the senior leader in their church, women were also not allowed to provide expertise in *any* area of the church. This is an unfortunate case where the church communicated only one side of the boundary line. They were clear about what a woman could *not* do, but didn't clarify what a woman *could* do.

Another example of needing to define boundaries is the topic of "office housework."[11] These are important tasks that keep everything running smoothly but are often not assigned to anyone specifically. Almost every leader we talked to and most of our survey participants mentioned the tension they feel around tasks that are usually labeled "women's work."

- "Why do they keep asking *me* to take the notes at the leadership meeting?"
- "The shared kitchen is a mess, but if I take time to clean it up, will that become my new role? Will it look as if I have extra time for something like that?"
- "Apparently I am the best one on this team of leaders to make an agenda and bring copies for everyone. Shouldn't the person running the meeting be doing that?"

Women often feel trapped between being willing to help where needed and falling into tasks that ultimately discredit their leadership clout. Not to mention, the more "housekeeping" a woman takes on, the less time she has to perform her real job. Establishing clear boundaries as leaders of what your "shared tasks" are and clearly rotating or assigning them will help keep your boundaries lined up with your values, and will be very relieving for the female leaders on your teams.

Boundaries really show up when someone is held accountable for violating them. This is especially important when trying to take on biases. Clearly defining how we will treat one another, regardless of gender, is an important conversation to have at all levels of the organization. But it becomes serious when people are held accountable for their actions, even to the point of termination. What we tolerate is what we believe. Tony Hsieh, CEO of Zappos, said, "We believe that it's really important to come up with core values that you can commit to. And by commit, we mean that you're willing to hire and fire based on them. If you're willing to do that, then you're well on your way to building a company culture that is in line with the brand you want to build."[12]

SYMBOLS AND ICONS

Symbols and icons carry deep meanings and can communicate much more effectively than words alone. If used intentionally, symbols carry significant power to influence and change culture. For example, adding a female to your senior leadership team is a very strong symbol of inviting women into leadership. There can also be unintentional symbols, however, such as having no women on the senior leadership team. Even if it is unintended, leaders will assume that females are not welcome to serve as leaders if they don't see any.

When I interviewed senior-level male church leaders about this topic, most of them talked about creating some strategic symbolic gestures to help communicate the new direction they wanted to go. This is definitely the place to start. Adding qualified and competent female leaders to your teams and projects and in significant leadership roles is an important and effective way to communicate change. Also, inviting women to speak, share their testimonies, or participate in a panel during a message can be very impacting, as can adding female speakers to any guest teaching plans you have at your church during the year.

However, numbers matter, and a symbolic gesture is just that . . . symbolic. Only putting one woman into a leadership position to give the appearance of gender equality is not the same as embracing diversity. The same is true for female speakers. As Verna Myers said, "Diversity is being invited to the party; inclusion is being asked to dance."[13] Only inviting a woman to speak one time a year on Mother's Day is not the same as embracing female communicators. That is known as tokenism and isn't helpful in the long term. The latest research has found that "diversity" has a threshold of 30 to 40 percent to be effective.[14] In other words, if you have ten ministry leaders, three to four of them should be female to be effective at gender diversity. If there are fifty-two sermons a year, it would be a very powerful statement if fifteen to twenty were taught by, or involved, a female.

For churches, the weekend worship service symbolizes much of what we believe and practice. We gather our whole church body together on the first day of the week to symbolize putting God first. We sing praises to Him, we worship together, we take the Lord's Supper to remember His sacrifice, we confess our sins, we greet one another, we bring our tithes, we study the Scriptures, we baptize new believers, we testify to what God has done, we celebrate miracles, and we share our burdens and prayer requests, among many other things. What we do as a church body at our weekend gatherings gets translated into how we operate as a faith community the rest of the week. It is our primary vehicle for communicating truth, vision, and culture.

One simple way to bring awareness to the value of women is

to include female biblical characters in your sermons. In my early twenties I started reading through the Bible every year. One of the most amazing realizations for me was how many incredible women are in Scripture. They led, they taught, they judged, they inspired, they failed, they influenced, they problem-solved, they discipled, and they were often hand-selected by God to be used in powerful and strategic ways. But for some reason, in most of the churches I've attended, they are rarely preached about.

Just in the last two weeks I've heard a sermon series on the book of Acts and a message about King Josiah's life. Unfortunately, both these pastors missed great opportunities to highlight the amazing female leaders in these scriptures—Priscilla and Huldah the prophetess. They simply skipped right over them when reading the texts and in the points of the messages. Women certainly don't need to be the central message every week, but I've found it is very easy and common with our current unconscious biases to simply skip over these sections of Scripture. The result is a biblical diet that is missing some key nutrients. I can only imagine what it would have been like as a young woman growing up in church to regularly hear how God uses women in His kingdom.

Almost all the churches I work with understand the power of symbols during weekend worship services when it comes to ethnic diversity. Most churches are trying to be more representative of the ethnic makeup of their communities by intentionally pursuing ethnically diverse musicians, singers, volunteer leaders, and staff members and to strategically include them onstage as part of weekend services. Pictures with multiple ethnic people are everywhere—programs, posters, banners, welcome signs. On more than one occasion I've seen a man of color attend his first church service and be pursued by multiple staff leaders that entire next week. When talking through candidates for a job, ethnic diversity is a strong preference. The same needs to happen for quality female leaders.

Making sure women are represented in our weekend services, in our publications, and in visible roles will help communicate the value of female leadership and that leadership is possible and encouraged for women. Celebrating female leaders, within the church and also within the community, will encourage and inspire young women to take advantage of leadership opportunities. This kind of affirmation sets them up to be much-needed mentors and coaches within your church body. Several of the female leaders we interviewed had their first leadership experiences on the worship team. Singing and leading music allowed them to become comfortable onstage and learn how to lead a congregation.

In addition, intentionally pursuing women to be a part of your leadership training and giving them "real jobs" with "real titles," even as volunteers, will be an important symbol to them, as well as the leaders who are watching.

PACING CHANGE

Creating a healthy, vibrant, and fruitful ecotone takes time. How much time? It depends on the environments and how open your people are to change—that's where the tension lies and where the potential is. In addition to the best practices we've outlined in the book, here are a few tips to keep in mind.

TALK THIS CHANGE THROUGH WITH THE MEN ON YOUR TEAMS.

The reality is, adding female leaders to your teams will change things. Even if everyone agrees that these changes are positive and the church will be better for it, it will *feel* different.

I remember my first campus pastors' meeting as their new leader. I walked in and they were in a giant wrestling pile in the middle of the room. Six grown men with flip-flops flying and laughter emanating. It was delightful, and although I did consider it for a half second, I decided I would not be able to be a part of that type of bonding, no matter how much I wished I could be.

These kinds of connections, memories, and bonding are part of what makes working together so much fun. But having only male-oriented types of bonding leads to all sorts of unintended consequences. Take some time with the men on your teams to talk about what those kinds of experiences might be like for the women of your church. Ask them what this must feel like, how they would respond if the tables were turned, and what they can do to help make it better.

One female leader suggested having the men on the team think through what it would be like if one of their most valued team members used a wheelchair. Would they still plan the annual golf day? Would they make decisions during a break in the men's room if their teammate had to use the handicap restroom down the hall? What other accommodations would they naturally want to make? How can you translate these ideas to be more welcoming to women on the team?

I've been the lone female on many teams, but I've also led teams of women and added a man. I have to say, being the one who has to incorporate a new voice, style, and perspective into a high-affinity team is much harder than being the one added. Everything seemed like it was easier before the new person arrived. Part of it was that we were an established team and had found our rhythm, but a big piece was that we easily clicked and moved like clockwork. We had added women on and off the team quite easily because they could quickly pick up our nuances and unspoken thoughts. It wasn't until we added a man that we realized we really could read each other's minds! But he brought a whole different energy, a new set of ideas, and connections with people that we never had before. To be honest, the friction was quite uncomfortable at times, but as the leader, I knew that it *was* worth it.

Press on and keep the vision of diversity, and its benefits, at the forefront. Move your friendship time to nonwork hours. Fewer inside jokes and a few more minutes to fully explain something in a meeting is well worth the trade-off in kingdom impact.

TALK THIS CHANGE THROUGH WITH THE WOMEN ON YOUR TEAMS.

As we've discussed earlier in this book, the women on your teams will likely have mixed emotions about these changes. Some will be thrilled, while others may actually be resistant. I have found that it is critical to lead your women with Scripture. Teach them. Help them wrestle with the theology for themselves. Give them books on the subject. Answer their questions. Allow them the time and space to think, pray, question, grieve, and dream.

The biggest resistance I have ever faced has been from women older than I am or married to the men with whom I work. Both are based in fear and usually got worked through by getting to know me and understanding my heart for serving as a leader. On the other hand, I have friends in church leadership who are seeing a new wave of young men and women be the more resistant ones. Talk through these issues not just in the theoretical but with the women who are actually leading.

Help them get to know one another and make space for the women who aren't sure if this is right, or at least may not be right for them. If you have women's groups or ministries, these would be important places to have conversations about your changing culture. Not everyone there will be leaders, but everyone there will have the ability to support or work against the female leaders you are adding to your teams.

In the interviews and survey, the topics of "girl hate," "catfights,"

"Queen Bee effect," and "women eat their young" all came up. Assuming women will be competitive and work against one another is not helpful and not necessary, especially in the kingdom. This is a bad cultural reputation that we need to reinvent. In fact, new research is indicating that these competitive behaviors are less about being female and more about being in an environment in which opportunities are scarce and highly competitive.[15] The more women are advancing in leadership, the more receptive our cultures are to females, and the more women talk through how to help one another, the better our cultures and our female relationships are becoming.

Talk with women about jealousy, coveting, anger, feeling left out, and what it means to know and pursue their calling. Reassure them that there is room for everyone and that you support all women in pursuing the calling God has on their lives. Cast a vision for unity, support, embracing change, and serving one another for the sake of the kingdom and for the benefit of your church.

LEAD YOUR LEADERS WELL.

Not everyone on your staff or in your church has had the opportunity to listen to the stories of your female leaders or process this change for as long as you and your leadership team have. Making assumptions about how people will respond will undermine trust and shut down the honest conversations that are needed to be a unified body.

Most leaders have found that it is helpful to lead with their theological positions. Take the time and effort to make your biblical case and explain how you arrived there. Assume your leaders love the Lord and want to do what is right in His eyes. You need to help them see the truth as you have discerned it. Take your time, spell it out, and then invite their questions and dialogue. To rush this process and demand compliance is to undermine a person's individual relationship with the Lord and that person's ability to hear from Him. Pray for your leaders, give them the resources they need to study the issue, be available as they process, and let God do His work.

At the end of the day, you will likely have some leaders and staff who will disagree with your theological position. You will likely even have some staff, volunteers, and members leave the church, but that's okay. At least they are leaving because of a difference in theology, not because of poor leadership. If you lead them through the process with love and faithfulness (Prov. 20:28), your relationships and your leadership will be fine, and likely stronger, on the other side.

Even in churches whose theology is very open to women leading at many levels, both male and female leaders talked about how their cultures are continuing to prevent women from growing and leading. Jon Ferguson, founding pastor of Community Christian Church in the Chicago area and cofounder of NewThing, an international movement of reproducing churches, told me he is surprised at the lack of progress for women leading in churches: "Without a doubt, there are more women in roles of significant influence in the church and nonprofits now than ever before. But the pace still feels really slow. I think in a lot of ways it does feel like two steps forward and one step backward."[16]

For their church specifically, he described not having a theological limitation on women in leadership but said, "Our unfortunate situation is that we tended to start out (as a church plant) male dominated. We had men in most of the positions of authority and that has continued much longer than we had hoped or would like. We are really recognizing that now, and it is something we are working hard on, and are making progress."[17]

HUMBLY CELEBRATE PROGRESS.

As with any kind of initiative or cultural shift, progress can sometimes feel slow. It is important to keep this vision alive in your teams and in your church, even if people's opinions are not moving as fast as you or some on your team would like. My advice is to stay humble, hopeful, and honest. Be up-front with your teams about the results you are seeing. Ask for prayer. Don't give up or acquiesce to those who are resistant. Continue to educate yourself and those around you.

If you keep the topic alive and in front of people, you take on the hardest part of unconscious bias—the unconscious part. Taking on your culture is probably the biggest and most important task in developing female leaders well. Embracing the tension inherent when two ecosystems come together is not easy, but it is necessary to have a richer and more fruitful community. By reevaluating your stated values and use of language, redefining borders, and integrating strategic symbols, you can help your culture shift to an environment that not only welcomes and supports new female leadership, but creates an opportunity for many more leaders to grow and thrive.

NEXT STEPS AND FINAL
THOUGHTS FOR CHURCHES

If you've done the hard work of defining your theology around the issue of women in leadership, then it's time to start taking some action to maximize the incredible talent and resources God has provided in your local body. Any of the best practices that have been outlined in this book will be helpful in moving you forward, but if you would like some practical first steps, here are ten to get you going.

START BY ASKING AND LISTENING

Begin with the female leaders you know and trust. Ask open-ended questions such as:

- "What is it like to be a woman leader at our church?"
- "How well are we stewarding your gifts for the enrichment of our church body?"
- "Where do you think our blind spots are when it comes to supporting female leaders?"

You can do this individually, in small discussion groups of two to three, or even in a more formal focus group of ten to twelve. I've found that a group of two to three gives the best opportunity for interaction and dialogue while keeping the conversation alive and giving everyone a chance to fully share their perspective. If you are not part of a bigger church, you can still pursue understanding with the female leaders you already know and minister with.

Give yourself plenty of time. In a group of two to three, I would set aside one and a half to two hours. For larger groups, allocate two to three hours. It usually takes this long to break through the surface "niceness" and get to the real meat of learning. Be intentional about setting up a relational and disarming environment. Include a meal or nice refreshments, or go to a restaurant with some privacy. Minimize distractions and interruptions. There will likely be some strong emotions and difficult experiences that will be shared, so you'll want to make sure everyone feels safe to do so without being overheard or made to feel awkward.

When inviting female leaders into these kinds of conversations, take a few minutes to be intentional about your invitation to share their perspectives. Remember: for most women this is a topic they have kept silent and "stuffed" for a while. You are giving them a wonderful gift, but not everyone will walk in ready to be real and vulnerable.

If possible, make the initial invitation personally, and let them know you want to learn how to do this better as a church and that their perspective would be very helpful in the process. Send them the questions ahead of time so they can think through them, recall real experiences, and have some space to process their emotions before discussing these things in a group setting. You can even encourage them to use some work time to think about the questions, prepare written notes, and process through any emotions they have before coming.

Assure them of the confidential nature of this conversation, how you intend to use this information, and that what they share will not be used against them now or in the future. It may seem obvious to you, but most women will wonder if participating and being fully honest are worth the risk.

As a leadership team, hold these "listening sessions" with women throughout your staff and volunteer leadership. Select "hosts" who are known for their trustworthiness and interpersonal skills. As senior and executive leaders, it is important that you are involved in this process and championing it from the top of the organization, but you also need to be honest about your own skills and abilities. You might want to recruit someone to facilitate the conversations, but it is still important that you are leading the initiative and staying informed of what they are learning.

It's also helpful to include several different women from different roles in the process. But be careful to not just talk to the women on your staff. You want to make sure you are talking to female leaders, so be sure to include female small group leaders, those who are leading with their husbands, and pastors' wives who are leading their own ministries, as well as staff people who are leading projects or teams.

When closing your conversation, thank each of the women for taking the risk and having the courage to be honest. Affirm their insights and commit to them that you will continue to reflect on what they've shared and pray about how you, as a church and a leadership team, can do better to support and value them and the women coming behind them. I know several pastors who have felt led to apologize to the women for the mistreatment they have experienced, even if those pasters weren't personally responsible for it. Take a moment to pray for the participants, the development and stewardship of their gifts, and God's call on their lives. Be sure to send a follow-up thank you as well.

When you have concluded your "listening sessions," decide as a team how you want to communicate your findings back to the participants and what you plan to do as a leadership team about these results. You don't need to feel pressure to meet anyone's expectations or do something drastic, but if these women have taken the risk to offer their insights and experiences, it is only respectable to return the favor by telling them how the process went, the basics of what you learned, and what next step they can expect to see from you. This also builds in some very healthy and important accountability. You might even consider telling them you hope they hold you accountable to making progress in this area. This builds a new level of trust, respect, and grace for the hard work of leading change.

No matter what role you have, whether or not you lead at a high level in your church, or even whether you are male or female, you can begin this kind of intentional learning and listening with the women you know and with whom you minister. Expand your understanding. Listen well. Take notes. Look for common themes or experiences. Ask follow-up questions. Restate what you are hearing to make sure you are understanding clearly and not jumping to conclusions or quickly connecting the dots from your own assumptions. You may just find out that you are doing better in some areas than you realized!

Keep an open mind and heart, ask the Lord to help you, and give the gift of your full attention. You will likely be the first person to ever ask these questions in this way, and that in itself will be quite encouraging and empowering.

DEFINE REALITY

Take some time to pull the basic HR metrics from Best Practice #7: Upgrade Your People Practices. Measure the first five and begin tracking these at least once a year as part of your annual personnel processes.

SET YOUR VISION, MILESTONES, AND GOALS

Now that you have gained some perspective and clearly defined where you are today, it is time to pray and dream about what God is calling you to in the future. You probably already have some exciting ideas, but dream together as a leadership team.

- What should our church look like in the future?
- Where could women add value and maximize their gifts?
- How do we see them influence and serve?
- What is missing today that can flourish in the future?
- How do we see men and women work more collaboratively?
- How will we get the best of everyone?

Next, begin to turn your vision into milestones. What would this look like ten years from now? Five years from now? One year from now?

Finally, begin to set some concrete goals. Although the metrics in #2 aren't the only thing you will look at, they are a quick and simple spot-check to make sure you are seeing real progress, not just talk and activity. It will also keep you from having only one or two strong, visible women leaders, but not creating space or a pathway to develop all your female leaders.

DESIGNATE A CHAMPION

Although there are many factors and teams that will contribute to moving the dial in your organization, there needs to be one person on the senior leadership team who is the "champion" and ultimately accountable for this initiative. This does three primary things:

1. It means someone wakes up every day and thinks about this topic. We all get busy, and if this were an easy initiative to implement, you probably would have done it already. Someone needs to carry the ball; otherwise the urgency of ministry will take over and you'll look at your metrics a year from now and realize you have not made much progress.

2. Designating a strong leader from your highest team tells everyone that this is important and is going to happen. It also gives the champion the authority to ask questions and speak into cross-departmental systems that need to be developed or changed.

3. It holds one person accountable for progress. If everyone is in charge, then no one is in charge. Promoting women in leadership should be an initiative that is a part of your regular accountability system, but it should also be reviewed by the leadership team regularly in the beginning to help build momentum and talk through any barriers, and then less frequently as you begin to make real progress. The champion will obviously be looking at the metrics often and bringing updates to the leadership team as needed.

LEAD YOUR LEADERS WELL

Take the time to talk through any theological changes with your leadership teams. Give them time to process and ask questions. See specific suggestions for doing this well in Best Practice #8: Take on Your Culture.

GIVE WOMEN VISIBILITY
AND PLATFORM

The organizational reality is that if you are visible, people assume you are a leader. Visibility on the weekend stage is a critical tool in communicating authority. When you extend the influence of the platform, you extend the influence of your leaders. Even if you are more conservative in your theological viewpoint, highlighting your female leaders on Sunday morning elevates their status in the congregation's mind, endorses the leadership you have given them, and helps people put a face with the name and ministry. Following are some suggestions on how you can begin to give women and your female leaders visibility.

- *Highlight your female leaders.* Bring them up during announcements, highlight what their ministry is doing, allow them to vision cast and celebrate what is happening under their leadership, affirm them, pray for them, and encourage the congregation to support them.
- *Tell positive stories about your female leaders.* Tell them in the sermon, at leadership gatherings and staff meetings, and during announcements.
- *Assign female leaders to give announcements.* This can seem silly, but even having a female leader or volunteer give the announcements on the weekend can be a big, visible symbol to the congregation.
- *Ask female leaders to lead staff and leadership meetings.* Give the women on your team the opportunity to open and close in prayer, lead the agenda, facilitate discussion, and give the updates. While you are at it, assign the guys to take the meeting notes and send out the calendar invites.

- *Recruit female leaders to teach or co-teach the membership class.* This is a great way to use women to teach about the history and beliefs of the church and why they love being a part of the church, and build relationships and connections with new attenders and their families. It communicates up front to every new person that women have a place and a voice in your church.
- *Give female leaders the opportunity to lead small groups and teach classes.* Be sure to use leaders who are knowledgeable and skilled. Giving women freedom to lead and teach classes about a variety of topics will build their skill sets and help change the mind-set of the congregation.
- *Ask female leaders to participate in a panel or team teaching.* This is a great way to introduce women onto the teaching platform. Mix up the weekend by interviewing a panel of people about their experiences or team teach a sermon with a female leader who is an excellent communicator. Avoid inviting women only to discuss the topics of being a wife and mom.
- *Bring in female guest speakers.* Bringing in a guest speaker is a great way to hear a woman's perspective and voice from your pulpit, especially if you are still building up the skill sets of your female communicators.

CLEAN UP BAD HABITS

We all have habits and ruts that we fall into in how we talk and portray ideas and people—and many are unintended. The best way to become more self-aware is to inspect your behavior and ask for accountability from others. As a team, you can do the same for one another.

For example, I recommend auditing your weekend services—or whatever your ministry or role—for how women are portrayed. It can be surprising how many times we send a message we didn't mean to send. Children and teenagers are especially vulnerable to their worldview being shaped by language and symbols. You might have a similar awareness if you were working on being more inclusive of people from a variety of socioeconomic levels, but discovered the only references in your sermon that week were about mortgage payments, standing in line at Starbucks, and that "new car smell." This is unintended, but unfortunate.

Here are some basic things you or someone on your team can start calculating. This doesn't have to feel negative or condemning; it is just making sure your culture (language, symbols, and boundaries) matches your values and beliefs.

- Number of times female leaders are highlighted from the stage (giving an example of a female in your church; announcing a female who is leading a class or event)
- Number of times a female actually leads on the stage
- Number of times teaching includes a positive reference to a biblical woman
- Number of times the primary example in the message is a strong female leader in the Bible
- Number of times inclusive-gender versus single-gender words are used (for example, using "people" instead of "mankind")
- Number of times a male leader authentically and positively references parental or household leadership (for example, a man picking up his kids from school or grocery shopping, especially in the context of this being a regular responsibility, not a onetime emergency or "favor" for his wife)
- Number of times a woman or a traditionally female responsibility is portrayed as negative or part of a joke

This is an area where you could set a goal of how many times you wanted to intentionally highlight women leaders positively in your service and eliminate negative references. Even highlighting women two to three times a Sunday over the course of a year could really change your culture. By the way, men are often portrayed in very negative ways as well: unable to parent effectively, addicted to sports, and generally dumb. This might be worth tracking as well. You can also look for how well you represent different ages and ethnic diversity.

BEGIN RECRUITING FROM THE PEWS

You might not have pews anymore, but there are likely strong, capable, and accomplished professional women in your church who could help raise the bar of your leadership and help move the needle on your diversity goals. Seek them out. Talk with them. Ask how your church is doing in speaking to their spiritual needs, ministering to them, and making space for them in ministry leadership.

As you listen and learn, look for women who are gifted and have a passion for your church, have a call to ministry, or are particularly interested in issues of gender equality. These are excellent leaders to begin recruiting for your leadership programs or next volunteer or staff role. You can even talk with them about your goals to position women in influential leadership roles who will provide strong examples and mentors for young leaders in your church. Many spiritually mature and seasoned female leaders will jump at the chance to take what they have experienced in their careers and bring it into ministry.

BE "OTHERS" INTENTIONALLY

In your top levels of leadership, discuss how every leader can personally come alongside the women on their teams or those with whom they have a natural connection. For example, look for similar gifts and abilities, type of work, area of passion, previous career, and so forth. Identify the top and most promising female leaders in your organization, identify what their strengths are and what the potential for them could be. Challenge each other on your biases, and be open to new ways of viewing people.

Brainstorm how you can sponsor your female leaders. What roles should be changed or created to give opportunities for your female leaders to grow and develop? Are there more formal systems and structures you could implement in your hiring and promotion processes to make sure women are given the same consideration as men?

Next, decide which staff leader is going to start connecting with each up-and-coming female leader. Agree upon a rhythm, a timeline, what should be happening during these mentoring moments, and how you will hold these leaders accountable. Many of these relationships will be a natural part of their leadership responsibilities already, but this will add intention and help create accountability for the development of your most promising female leaders. It will also help make sure someone who knows and feels responsible for the person is regularly sponsoring your female leaders for projects, opportunities, and promotions. Not every connection will be fantastic, but you will certainly communicate value and give some great opportunity for everyone to learn and become better at mentoring across gender lines.

Be sure to use your organizational chart so that every female leader is on the list. You want to start at the top of your organization and work your way down to create a level of trust and understanding of how people are being prioritized for this effort. Be up-front with your staff about what you are doing and why. You'll want to make sure you speak to a mind-set of "room for everyone" and eliminate any sense of favoritism, competition, or exclusion.

If you are in an environment without a lot of seasoned female ministry leaders, be sure to offer to pay for leadership coaching from an outside source. Although internal mentors and sponsors are critical, a female leader who can address the issues that are unique to women will also be very helpful, communicate how much you value female leaders, and acknowledge that there are some things they deserve that you aren't able to offer yet from within your organization.

IMPLEMENT GIFT-BASED MINISTRY PLACEMENT

Helping women identify their spiritual gifts is a critical step in leading them to embrace their calling in your church. There are several ways to do this and some comprehensive systems you can implement; however, it doesn't have to be complicated. Simply adding a spiritual gifts assessment to your volunteer sign-up process or your membership class can add a new dimension of spiritual growth to your people and increase the effectiveness of your volunteer teams. It introduces the concepts and biblical language of spiritual gifting and connects that to a person's contribution in your ministry.

In addition to starting from the bottom up, begin introducing gift-based ministry or refreshing this with your leaders. Take your team through their own gift assessments. Discuss the different strengths and weaknesses each person brings to the team. Talk about what perspective is missing in your decisions. What gifts are not being used fully? Who is working primarily outside their giftedness? This is a great leadership conversation to have in general, but it also helps introduce the idea of gift-based ministry and takes gender out of the equation. You will likely have many people who have unrealized gift potential that you'll want to utilize differently moving forward, including some women who have leadership, teaching, administration (not to be confused with *administrative* skills), or other traditionally non-female gifts that you'll be able to talk about and celebrate. It also helps leaders begin to recruit and train for roles on their teams based on giftedness versus bias.

These are just ten suggestions, but you know your organization and your culture better than anyone. Just begin with something. As someone has said, "The secret to getting ahead is getting started." If you haven't clearly defined your theological position yet, you should be working on that, but you can also begin highlighting the women you already have leading. There are women and girls in the congregation who will notice the difference and see the Lord, and themselves, in a bigger and more beautiful light. I can't wait to see how God will use them.

MY FINAL THOUGHTS FOR YOU

My pastor concluded the moment with, "This is what heaven will look like."

I remember it as if it were yesterday. It was one of the most significant ministry moments I have ever experienced. I had recently joined our church's staff team at a time when God's hand was clearly moving in the lives of people in unique ways. I loved praying with people at the altars after weekend services, but this evening's service was different. For the first time, we had people accept Christ in five different languages almost simultaneously: English, Spanish, Portuguese, Haitian, and sign language.

Listening to these prayers around me touched my heart in a special way. It awoke something in me that this white, middle-class, Montana girl had not experienced before or was even aware was missing from my life and faith: diversity.

Since that night, I have continued to pray for, look for, and embrace experiences and relationships with people who are different from me in all sorts of ways—ethnic backgrounds, physical abilities, ages, professions, belief systems, socioeconomic levels, perspectives, geographical locations, and political views. I'm frustrated to admit that this has been harder to do than I thought it would be. I'm also ashamed that I am far more uncomfortable in these situations and have more biases than I would like to admit. And if I am being brutally honest, chief among my own mysterious and unexpected biases is the one I often have had against other women.

I am embarrassed to admit how long it has taken me to fully embrace and appreciate a female news anchor, trust a female physician, or consistently listen to female-hosted podcasts or television shows. I've seen myself in those "likability" statistics, and I'm saddened to think that I have helped, in any way, propagate the status quo for women, especially in ministry settings. I feel as if this pursuit has been a mixture of repentance, wandering, learning, risking, and hoping that I am getting better at not letting fear sabotage what God has for me and those I serve.

Fear is a deceitful and powerful blinder. It causes us to forget that there's always room for one more at God's table. It causes us to believe that our amazing gifts are diminished by the brilliant gifts of someone else. And it causes us to overlook that there will always be more than enough people to love, more than enough people to serve, more than enough people with whom we can share the gospel, and more than enough people who need great leadership. In God's kingdom, there is more than enough for all of us.

Why are we afraid to share? Why are we afraid to step into our calling with others who are fully stepping into theirs? I have a suspicion that wrapping our heads and hearts around the gender issue will help us answer these questions and unlock other solutions.

Almost every church I know is working to be more ethnically diverse, but it seems to always be just out of reach. Could it be that if we were to embrace listening to women's viewpoints and experiences, we would be better at welcoming and embracing diversity of all kinds? If we were able to fully include women, who already make up more than half of our church attendance, into leadership, would we be more ready to share our leadership with people who truly are minorities? Something to ponder and watch for.

But I sense a great hope for change. The conversation is shifting. Leaders are taking notice. Sometimes it's because of something personal, such as a talented daughter coming of age and asking, "Dad, is there a place for me in the church you pastor?" Sometimes a moral or spiritual crisis forces a church team to look deeper at what is really going on behind closed doors. Other times it's based on principle, like the white men and white celebrities who took part in the civil rights movement's March on Washington because when the people with the power start taking up the plight of the powerless, those watching from the sidelines start to have their long-standing paradigms shifted.[1] May we see it again.

Overall, there has been a general sense, even among the male leaders I've talked to, that as the church, we know we are called to do better. We should be leading the way on these issues and setting the moral standard for the rest of the world, not learning from their research and being challenged by their morality.

Today, in our generation, there are 70 million women currently participating in America's churches.[2] If each of those women simply volunteered one additional hour a month, that is an additional 840 million volunteer hours unleashed in our ministries *every year*. Whatever your church's next step is, you have an incredible opportunity to develop women's gifts and skills for the kingdom as never before. What could be different in the life of your ministry and mission if you began to unleash the potential of the female leaders already in your midst?

For churches opening this dialogue, perhaps for the first time: I want to applaud your courage and cheer you on to pursue all that God has for your church. Seek God's truth and you can't go wrong.

For churches unsatisfied with how they steward the gifts and abilities of their female leaders: I want to encourage you that even small moves toward empowerment can go a long way. Having honest conversations, giving the female leaders you already know a voice and platform, and teaching how God has used women for kingdom impact can spark a passion in a female leader that you'll get to harness, nurture, and celebrate.

For those successful churches that already have influence and platform: I want to encourage you to lead the way. Like those white businessmen, pastors, politicians, and celebrities in the March on Washington, you have an opportunity to open up doors of influence for not only the women on your teams but the women in churches around the world. Continue to learn and work on this issue at home, but also speak about it when you are connecting with other leaders. Raise the level of dialogue in your tribes. Invest in female leaders and use the platforms God has given you to create pathways for change. You hold the keys to unlock their potential.

And for the male leaders who are tackling this issue in your circles of influence: Thank you. Thank you for seeing us. Thank you for caring. Thank you for praying. Thank you for believing that there is more to be gained together than apart. Thank you for opening doors, both figuratively and literally. Thank you for dealing with your own issues in a way that doesn't hold us back. Thank you for being open. Thank you for taking the risk. Thank you for being a living example of losing your life (Matt. 16:25), being last (Mark 10:31), and laying down your life for a friend (John 15:13). We are eternally grateful.

I had the privilege of interviewing Dr. Jo Anne Lyon for this book project. Although in her seventies, she is currently the general superintendent emerita and ambassador of the Wesleyan Church, after leading the denomination for several years as the first female general superintendent. She has served in pastoral ministry for more than thirty years, has been granted five honorary doctorates, and is the founder and CEO of World Hope International, which serves in more than thirty countries to alleviate suffering and injustice. She is my new hero.

Jo Anne believes that God is calling more women than He ever has before. In her studies of historical theology, she explained that every time there has been a spiritual awakening, women are often called up into ministry and spiritual leadership. It's one of the signs of a revival that isn't talked about very often.

But within the United States, she explained, there has been an unfortunate cycle. Historically, when a spiritual awakening begins to take place, we tend to want to organize it. To administrate it. To systematize and institutionalize it. In the process, the women tend to be pushed out. But she believes, "We are in the midst of a new awakening, and God is calling women like never before. And I'm praying that this time the women will *stay* engaged. The movement is taking place!"[3]

What if this is true? What if the rise of female leaders we seem to be seeing all around us is a sign that God is finally answering the prayers of 2 Chronicles 7:14 that many of us have been praying for, for years?

> If my people who are called by my name will humble themselves, and pray and seek my face, and turn from their wicked ways, then I will hear from heaven, and will forgive their sin and heal their land.

What if this is what we are seeing? I pray so. And I pray that, this time, we will not miss out.

After all, this *is* what heaven will look like.

TEAM DISCUSSION QUESTIONS

BEST PRACTICE #1: SEEK TO UNDERSTAND

1. What kinds of gender roles did you grow up with? How did you respond to them?
2. How have you seen women be conditioned from our society or churches?
3. Do you think your church has a "stained glass ceiling"? What have you observed that supports your view?
4. Have you ever observed a leader struggle with a "sticky floor" (his or her own behaviors or perspectives are holding that leader back)? What can you do to help women overcome this?
5. Who are some female leaders you could begin asking about their leadership journey?

BEST PRACTICE #2: CLEARLY DEFINE WHAT YOU BELIEVE

1. How clear is your understanding of your church's theological lines for female leaders in your church? Do you think others on your team have this same level of clarity?

2. Saint Augustine said, "In essentials, unity; in non-essentials, liberty; in all things, charity." From your perspective, does this topic qualify as an "essential" or a "nonessential"?

3. Looking at the theological chart, where would you plot your beliefs growing up? Your beliefs now? Your church's beliefs?

4. On a scale of 1 to 5, how aligned do you think the daily practices throughout your church's culture are with your theological beliefs?

5. What next steps does your team need to take to bring more clarity and consistency to this topic?

BEST PRACTICE #3: MINE THE MARKETPLACE

1. Who are some of the marketplace leaders (male or female) contributing in your ministry?

2. How well are you, as a church or team, leveraging the marketplace to access successful female leaders? What improvements can you make?

3. Have you ever been guilty of recruiting quality female leaders but not giving them "real jobs" with fair pay? What underlying philosophy or policy informed that decision?

4. How are you utilizing corporate worship services and other influential platforms to help demonstrate your beliefs about female leaders?

5. How are you helping female leaders transition into ministry, including supporting their husbands and families?

BEST PRACTICE #4: INTEGRATE SPIRITUAL FORMATION AND LEADERSHIP DEVELOPMENT

1. How well does your church integrate spiritual growth and leadership development? For men? For women?

2. Are you missing any opportunities to develop female leaders in your current discipleship programs? What could you do differently?

3. What is your reaction to the idea that, in our culture, men become more likable as they advance in leadership but women become less likable? Why do you think this happens?

4. In the Heidi/Howard résumé experiment, changing a first name altered how someone's abilities were perceived. Describe a time when you've caught yourself having this type of bias.

5. How well does your church help people identify their spiritual gifts and connect those gifts in serving opportunities? Where could you make improvements for women in this process?

BEST PRACTICE #5: BE AN "OTHER"

1. What "others" have played a significant role in your life and leadership? How?

2. How does your church's informal networks help up-and-coming male leaders? Do female leaders get these same experiences?

3. What are your thoughts about the "missing 33 percent"? Are there ways your leadership systems are leaving out critical pieces of development for female leaders?

4. On a scale of 1 to 5, how well are your church's top leaders mentoring female leaders? How about sponsoring female leaders? Providing experienced female coaches?

5. Do you agree that most female leaders on the staff team carry a double shift? Are there ways your church could provide benefits to all employees that would strategically support female leaders who carry a double shift?

BEST PRACTICE #6: CREATE AN
ENVIRONMENT OF SAFETY

1. What has been your experience with either sexual abuse or immorality at work or church? How has this impacted you?
2. What's your response to the idea that the Billy Graham Rule needs to be expanded to fit our day and culture? In your culture, what are some adaptations you can make to be protective but inclusive of the women on your team?
3. How well do you think people in your church understand the levels of intimacy and how this should play out in healthy and safe relationships?
4. How can you adjust your personal leadership practices to be able to offer equal opportunities to both men and women whom you lead or influence?
5. What assumptions need to be challenged in your church culture to make sure both male and female leaders can be developed fully?

BEST PRACTICE #7: UPGRADE
YOUR PEOPLE PRACTICES

1. Have you ever thought much about bias before? What do you think of the research that concluded that the more strongly one believes he or she has no biases, the more likely that person is to exhibit biased behavior?
2. What stood out to you in the section about female leaders generally not getting equal pay and benefits for the same work? Has your church ever been guilty of this?
3. Do the titles in your team or church accurately describe the responsibilities and authority given to each person? Are you seeing any unintended consequences when these don't match?
4. How well does your church give regular and honest feedback to female leaders? What has been the result of this?

5. What are the most important metrics for your church to start measuring? What do you hope this will accomplish?

BEST PRACTICE #8: TAKE ON YOUR CULTURE

1. How big of a shift will it be for your culture to begin doing a better job developing female leaders? What will likely be the biggest area of resistance?
2. How well does your team fully listen to a woman's thoughts and perspectives? Have you ever engaged in or experienced "manterrupting"?
3. Verna Myers said, "Diversity is being invited to the party; inclusion is being asked to dance." What do you think of this quote? How are female leaders "invited" into leading in your church? How are they "asked to dance" in leading in your church?
4. Are there strategic symbolic moves you could make that would highlight female leaders in your culture?
5. How fast is your church culture able to change? What are the most important steps you can take to pave the way to changing your culture to be better at developing female leaders?

NEXT STEPS AND FINAL THOUGHTS FOR CHURCHES

1. What do you think about the idea that embracing gender diversity might help your church do a better job with ethnic diversity?
2. From the suggested list of "next steps," which one do you think is the *most* important to tackle in the next thirty days?
3. When it comes to developing female leaders, where do you hope your church could be in five years?

BEST PRACTICES FOR
FEMALE LEADERS

I set out to write this book specifically for churches and church leadership teams because, after all, they hold most of the keys to unlocking the development of female leaders. But, as women, we also hold a few keys ourselves, and I just couldn't send this project out into the world without capturing some of the incredible thoughts and advice from the amazing women whom I interviewed and those who participated in our survey. Their insights are full of godliness, wisdom, wit, intelligence, reality, humor, and love for others being called to travel up the same path. I hope the Lord opens up many opportunities for all of us to sit together, share stories, and learn, encourage, and sharpen one another—sooner rather than later!

But in the meantime, here is a quick overview of the top five best practices that emerged, a few of my personal learnings thrown in for fun, as well as some final words of wisdom uncovered from our interviews. May they get you started on the right path and fuel you as you take on all that God has for you.

BEST PRACTICE #1: GET CLEAR
ON YOUR CALLING

Figuring out my calling has always been much harder for me than it seemed to be for others. I'm not exactly sure why, but now that I'm older and have a bit more perspective, I'm starting to think it may have to do with a combination of seemingly competing internal priorities:

- Honoring both the intended and unintended messages I received growing up in my particular hometown, family, church, and friends.
- A set of natural gifts and abilities I loved exercising.
- My desire to honor God and obey Him wholeheartedly.
- Striving for a Jesus-like servant's heart in which I would joyfully sacrifice personal comfort for the sake of loving others well.
- Participating in the lifelong process of sanctification in which I keep learning just how sinful and screwed up I am. My heart has a tendency to wander into unhealthy spaces of codependency, perfectionism, insecurity, gluttony, loneliness, and fear.
- A burden to not only steward but maximize the opportunities God has given me.

I think this is why I'm so passionate about Coaching and Life Planning. I know what it feels like to wander and I know what it feels like to be on mission. Being on mission is much better, and so I want to help people get to that clarity faster.

But discerning your calling is also a journey that God unfolds as you walk with Him and navigate life's twists and turns. Part of my personal story has been navigating what felt like a ten-year hiatus from my calling. After my husband was seriously injured in a twenty-five-foot fall at work, my life took a sharp and unexpected turn away from what I thought was my calling to be a stay-at-home mom of a gaggle of kids. I was pregnant at the time and spent the next several years going to rehab appointments and caretaking my husband through three surgeries. When his injuries didn't heal, and his pain worsened, I eventually went back to work full time to support our family so he could concentrate on his recovery. The gaggle of kids turned out to be an only child, and I went from a stay-at-home mom to a full-time executive leader and caretaker. I essentially became a single parent trying to help a little boy have some sense of normal childhood in the midst of daily family crises.

The kicker is that I spent the better part of my twenties trying to surrender my desire to be a career woman. I love working, or rather, I love accomplishing. If I were a millionaire I'd still be busy, talking leadership and ministry all day long and most of the night. I constantly have eight to ten books that I'm reading at one time; none of them fiction. I love learning from interesting people, and I'm constantly planning how I can work with them to do something extraordinary. At any one time I have a dozen new ideas bopping around in my head. It has taken me years to learn that my summer vacation is not the time to launch a new business or ministry venture, even if I feel like I suddenly have a lot of time on my hands.

As you can probably guess, that ten-year hiatus wasn't really a hiatus. It wasn't a detour, or even unexpected. It was part of how God was refining my calling. These new, unwanted limitations on my time, energy, and capacity were not roadblocks to overcome, but guardrails God had set up to help me refine my priorities, my greatest contribution, and what He ultimately planned to do in and through my life. The valley of the shadow of death had a way of working out my perfectionist tendencies. Who has time for perfection when you're just trying to survive?

When everyone I felt I needed was stripped away and it was

just me and God, I began to understand in my deepest soul from where my strength really comes. I remember months of waking up every morning desperately asking God for a miracle that day, and He would give it. When the basic responsibilities of my life became overwhelming, I had to give up my precious identity of being a "rescuer." My biggest regrets were when I stepped in and did more than God asked me to do. That's all on me. I needed the tough lessons of listening and obeying, rather than merely assessing and solving. Stewarding an abundance of ability, it turns out, is much harder than maximizing a shortage.

Tough lessons. But suffering is the gateway to sanctification, and at the end of the day, isn't that what we know to be the ultimate goal? Not to *do* like Jesus, but to *be* like Him? That is the center of calling: not to do in order to be, but to be *with* Jesus in order to do *with* Jesus. Out of being flows doing—the doing of all our callings, whatever they may be.

The key is to know this from the Lord, directly. Other people help, but at the end of the day, most of us are going to have a Daniel moment. There will be an opportunity to obey God alongside an opportunity to be applauded by other people. How can we choose God if we don't know for sure that it's Him? Here are the top ways to get clear on your calling from our female leaders.

1. FEAST ON GOD'S WORD

Engage in the conversation God wants to have with you through His Word. This isn't about studying for a seminary class or preparing for a team devotional but about your devotion to Him. That personal, intimate, soul-satisfying direction that you receive only when you humbly and prayerfully open up God's Word and listen for His voice. It's praying God's Word out loud over your life, ministry, and the people you love. It's memorizing scriptures that equip you for spiritual battle. And it's worshipping God through studying and learning simply for the sake of building your love and connection with Him. *He* is our great reward, nothing else.

"Do not be afraid, ____[*your name*]____. I am your shield, your very great reward." (Genesis 15:1)

This is also where you need to wrestle *for yourself* your beliefs about what you should or should not be doing. No one else can answer this for you. Do the work. Study, read, pray, ponder, discern, discuss, question, challenge, and then decide; or at least decide to keep pushing toward an answer.

I think many of us are still leaning in, trying to discern and hear what God wants to tell us. A lifelong belief system is hard to undo, but truth does set us free. And being set free by God himself is the freedom that allows us to hear and obey our calling.

2. EMBRACE BEING A MISFIT

What great biblical leader wasn't a misfit in their time and place? Leaders, by definition, don't fit in. They go first. They see things others can't see yet. The fallenness of this life bothers them more than it does other people—that's why they are the ones who do something about it. If they fit in, are laissez-faire, or think like everyone else, then they are following, not leading.

For me it took practice to be able to stand alone. As an introvert, I loved being by myself at home, but when in public, where people could *see* that I was by myself, my insecurities would take over, and I'd come up with all sorts of stories in my head of what people might be thinking about me: *She must not have any friends. Something must be wrong with her. How sad that she's all by herself.*

This was an issue for me in high school. I actually don't think I ate in the lunchroom the entire four years. At first I went home for lunch, but after a few weeks I figured out I could join extracurricular clubs that met during lunch. I was in five clubs my freshman year, one for each day of the week.

As Christians, standing alone is required, and especially as leaders. Learning how to confidently stand where we are supposed to be, without the need to defend ourselves or put others down, is part of the overflow of our deep understanding of who we are in Christ. If our identity is built in Him, being a misfit makes sense because He was a misfit. We are standing alone when we take on that new responsibility, or turn down that opportunity, or speak up, or say no. We stand against the pressures, the scripts, or the assigned roles. We disappoint people. But we obey what God is calling us to do, regardless of the cost. As long as we are doing that, we will be misfits until heaven. That's when we'll finally fit in. That is the hope that anchors our soul.

3. STEWARD YOUR GOD-GIVEN GIFTS

Knowing yourself, what you are gifted to do, and how you go about using those gifts to serve others is foundational to understanding your calling. Your gifts don't necessarily spell out *what* you do, but they help you know *how* to go about doing it.

For example, my primary gifts are administration, teaching, and encouragement. That means that no matter what opportunity God calls me to, these are the primary ways He is expecting me to fulfill my responsibilities. So, when I was asked to lead the young adult ministry, I organized it and built a team, taught some of the classes, and encouraged people to take their next step of faith. When I ran the First Impressions Teams, where we greet newcomers, I brought organization, teaching, and encouragement to those teams because those are my gifts. It was the same with launching campuses, building a leadership school, and writing this book.

My hope is that through this book I've organized the concerns around gender roles and ministry leadership in ways that are now clearer and easier to understand, and that my readers have learned something along the way and are encouraged to take the next step, whatever that may be. This would mean that my gifts have been used to serve and help others. My gifts also impact my other callings—how I parent, and the kind of wife, daughter, sister, neighbor, and friend I am. All my callings and my gifts will have a place in each of these roles.

Knowing my gifts also means that it doesn't matter if the guy before me was a more entrepreneurial/apostolic leader who started lots of things or had a gift of knowledge and could share a devotional thought that would have my head spinning for days. I'm not him. I'm me. And God has called me to use my gifts in this role at this time. To try to be someone else is to miss what God wants to do now through me. Leadership is personal because how I lead is an expression of who God has made me to be.

This doesn't mean I don't grow and learn. In fact, it is very important that I take ownership of the development of my gifts. When I get to heaven, God is going to ask what I did with what I was given. He's not going to ask my boss or my husband or my pastor. He is going to ask me. (He will have different questions for them.)

Learn everything you can about your gifts. Who in the Bible leads with those gifts? How does God speak to someone with those gifts? What are His expectations? When has someone misused them and what did that look like? Who in your community have those gifts? What do you see in them that you admire? What do you want to stay away from? What books can you read? What trainings can you go to? How can you get feedback? How can you grow and become better?

Get affirmation from people you trust and admire. What you love to do is one thing, what you are fruitful at doing can sometimes be something quite different. If you aren't sure of what I'm talking about, just think for a moment about those *American Idol* auditions where someone who *loves* to sing is actually terrible at singing.

If we're not careful, this can happen to us. Sometimes what we *desire* to be can be so clear that we lose sight of who we really are *created* to be. This is where godly, trustworthy people come in. Spiritual gifts are meant to be affirmed by the spiritual community you are a part of. If your church doesn't have a formal process for gift-based serving, then ask people to give you feedback. Tell them what gifts you think you might have and ask if they've seen those gifts in you produce any spiritual fruit.

Fruit is the key. Having skills or forcing yourself to become competent may require honorable self-discipline, but you're looking for fruit of the Spirit, which is a totally different thing. Where is God's anointing showing up in your life and ministry? Where is your minor effort producing major results? Oftentimes spiritual gifts seem so natural that you may not even realize not everyone else can do what you can do. Ask around, be open to feedback, get lots of opinions and examples, and then see where God is blessing your efforts.

The flip side of taking ownership of your gifts is taking responsibility for their down sides. As you study your giftedness, look for its shadow side. We all have them. When my gifts run amuck I can be controlling, bossy, and quick to judge. I also tend to overexplain and avoid calling out bad behavior. I don't mean to, and I certainly don't want to, but knowing this about myself keeps me in tune with my behavior and in check around my biggest temptations. It also helps me warn people about my dark side and invite open and helpful feedback. We all need other people to tell us when we are not being Christlike, because self-awareness first comes from others' feedback.

Knowing what your best contribution is helps free you from trying to be someone you're not. Who wouldn't love being an incredible vocalist who can usher people into the presence of God through music and prayer? Or preach a message that brings thousands to Christ? I know I would. But my fourth grade choir director helped me accept early on that singing was not my main gift. I'll admit, it was a little crushing at the time, and I secretly still belt out some serious praise and worship songs alone in my car on a long drive. But if I had spent the last thirty years pursuing music instead of leadership, I would have missed out on so much. God's plan won't be thwarted, but I certainly don't want to miss out on anything He wants me to be a part of.

"For if you remain silent at this time, relief and deliverance will arise from another place . . . And who knows but that you have come to your royal position for such a time as this?" (Esther 4:14)

4. ALWAYS SAY "YES!"

These were consistent themes in the interviews: Take advantage of every opportunity given to you. Do multiple things at once. Experiment. Push yourself. Don't be afraid to add to your plate. Take on big challenges. If God is calling you to it, He will equip you to do it. It may cause you to prioritize differently, lead at a higher level, and get rid of things in your life that are lower on the priority list, but these are all good things God probably wants you to do anyway.

Of course, I say this within reason. If your boss or some other key person in your life (including the Lord) is telling you *not* to do something, be respectful and obedient. But if there are no clear boundaries holding you back, do not hold yourself back, especially if you are early on in your leadership. Push yourself to explore and investigate opportunities. Don't wait for someone to give you permission or for the clouds to miraculously part. Start looking and asking God to open doors and bring to light where He wants you to focus your efforts.

I remember wishing I had an opportunity to teach. I was in an environment where teaching positions for women were not common, but I knew I had a gift and I knew I wasn't using it. I longed to become better at teaching, but that's difficult without practice. I took it to the Lord and told Him that if He gave me this gift, He must want me to use it, but I was good with His ways and His timing. I promised that whatever opportunities He brought me, I would say yes, no matter what they looked like. And I did.

The first opportunity to come my way was to lead a small group in my neighborhood. It was video based, but at least I got to lead the discussion. The second opportunity came a year later, to speak at a local mom's group. The third one a few months after that, to give the welcome and announcements at our newly launched campus. Then the fourth, to speak at a pastors' conference in my hometown for the wives. I couldn't believe it! That one really pushed me.

I felt like I was on my way, but it was followed by four years of absolutely nothing. Then I was on the stage at our new church giving announcements every week and speaking at our women's gatherings, and later I got a new job and was teaching quite frequently in our School of Leadership. Now I speak at conferences and workshops a couple times a month. It's taken fifteen years, but God has been growing my skill sets. I still say yes, and most of the time I wonder how in the world I will ever be able to pull it off. But then somehow God steps in and helps me to figure it out.

Even if all you can commit to is being a part of a network or board or team, get involved. You don't have to be the top leader or do anything crazy amazing, but you need to keep your networks alive and your gifts in play. This is especially helpful during early motherhood when it is easy to let those things go.

5. DON'T HOLD BACK

"Iris, in the movies we have leading ladies and we have the best friend. You, I can tell, are a leading lady, but for some reason you are behaving like the best friend." (Arthur Abbott in the movie, *The Holiday*[1])

I love this quote because I feel like this has been my life: the best friend, the second chair, the supporter, the celebrator, the equipper, the second choice, the vice-whatever. In many ways I think my male-dominated church environment was the perfect place for me to contribute in a significant way, but also to nurture my tendency to avoid the spotlight and the vulnerability that comes with it; no one photographs your flaws when you're hiding in the wings.

I didn't start out that way, and in fact I'm starting to think I was made for center stage. (Insert eye rolls from my closest friends.) But somewhere along the way to young adult womanhood, working to build a godly marriage, living in Christian environments of the South, listening to a few too many negative voices in my inner circle, and being in a church system that gave me all sorts of mixed messages about what it means to be a strong female, I pulled back. I started to spiritualize being "less than."

In the midst of that, God still forced me to be "more than," but I didn't go after it. I didn't even really want it. Regardless, it's where I found myself, so I stepped back into the light. It was uncomfortable at first because I received a lot less applause and a lot more criticism than I did while serving from the shadows. But God demanded that I figure out the difference between humility and settling. It was a painful but important distinction.

The Israelites had a similar experience. After crossing the Red Sea and spending way too long in the wilderness, they found themselves on the edge of the promised land. That journey was full of wandering and questioning and flat-out sinning. But before them stood the spotlight of center stage: three hundred thousand square miles of promised land in which they would bless and influence the entire world.[2] Yes, there were battles to be fought and a giant river to be crossed, at harvest time no less, and their longtime leader was not going with them. But God was half-inviting and half-demanding that they move out of the shadow and into their calling. This is where faith is lived out, in the space between what is and what could be.

Unfortunately, the Israelites didn't conquer their tendency to settle. It's a lesson they never learned. They battled and fought and claimed thirty thousand square miles as their new homeland—a mere 10 percent of what God had set aside for them.[3]

I don't want that to be me, and I certainly don't want that to be you. God has ordained ground for you to claim, places for you to be victorious, and a positioning in which you will bless and influence your world. It doesn't have to look a certain way or involve any sort of milestone or achievement. One of my favorite "leading lady" roles right now is leading a small group of five middle school girls on Sunday mornings. It doesn't have to be flashy to be significant. For most of us, our three hundred thousand square miles won't even be seen until heaven. I've lived at only 10 percent, and although I enjoyed it and learned from it, I don't want to leave any more ground unclaimed. I want to conquer all the places God has ordained for me, big and small.

If you are prayerfully pursuing your calling, you are a leading lady. Let's not live like anything less.

BEST PRACTICE #2: KNOW YOUR ENVIRONMENT

As much as I wish it were not so, the reality is, the environment you're in will greatly impact how you're able to lead and what opportunities will be given to you. And it's that way within any profession or organization, not just in churches.

But make no mistake: God's plans for you cannot be stopped. He may use times of rich environments or times of desert environments to do His great work in your heart. Our interviews and survey comments were overrun with hindsight appreciation for all that God had taught and did through seasons of limitations and challenges. But wrestling through the reality of your environment and praying through whether God wants you to be there is another whole process. Here are some important questions to ask as you discern where God wants you to serve.

1. IS YOUR HEART RIGHT?

Keeping a spirit of unity, respect, and submission is always going to be asked of you. We all serve under authority, so honoring the roles God has established will always win in the end. You can be strong, smart, confident, and vocal without being disrespectful. Speaking out from a place of humble strength that asserts your rights is very different from lashing out, exhibiting passive-aggressive behavior, or engaging in destructive gossip. In cases of abuse or ungodly behavior or treatment, however, you are under no obligation to defend or endure under that kind of environment.

2. DO YOUR BELIEFS LINE UP?

Rarely do one's beliefs fully line up with those of every other person in their church. So focus on the major things and look past the minor things. But if the issue of women leading in the church is an important topic for you, or if it impacts how you will fulfill your calling, you need to know *for yourself* what you believe God is saying about this. Then, you need to know what your church believes about this. If they match, great! It makes things very easy and peaceful.

But if they don't match up, you need to decide if you can live within those belief systems and support them as a part of the church. Staying but consistently challenging or disagreeing is not an option. Many people stay within the church systems in which they don't agree on every single point, and that's fine. The key is, you have to be able to support your leadership, respect its views, and communicate them, especially if you hold any sort of leadership position.

For what it's worth, I've seen this happen at all sides of the theological spectrum. It truly is okay to stay, and it's also okay to go. There is no clear right or wrong answer here. There's just you, your family, your church, and what faith community God is leading you to be a part of for the next season.

The only exception would be if your church is in the process of figuring out, or clearly articulating, what they believe. This can be a tough process. It's reasonable to give your leaders plenty of space and time to arrive at their best conclusion and discernment of what God has for your community. In the meantime, offer your perspective and helpful information with humility and pray for God to speak and lead them clearly.

3. ARE YOU ABLE TO FOLLOW YOUR LEADERS?

A final piece of knowing your environment comes down to the actual leaders in place. I've seen churches that seem to have everything going for them, except that either the senior pastor or one of the top leaders is "off" just enough that everything gets wonky. Sometimes God leaves us in places that are tough, and other times He releases us to move on to healthier teams and churches. Working through your emotions and experiences can help you identify the underlying issues, so you can decide if they are big enough to cause you to make a change. One of my good friends worked for a senior pastor who was very difficult, and the situation was getting worse every year. She hung in there, probably longer than she should have, because she loved the people and was holding out hope that things would turn around. Eventually she had to leave, because of what his poor leadership was doing to her personally and spiritually.

I, too, had an experience working for a pastor who had very little insight into his own gifts and abilities. Because of this he tended to operate out of the flesh rather than the spirit and wanted the rest of us to gut it out with him, regardless of our wiring or giftedness. Eventually, I had to move on, because I felt called to steward and develop my own gifts. Either he couldn't see the value in helping me develop my gifts, or he simply didn't know how to help me. I've also worked for incredibly gifted and godly leaders who, even in the midst of tighter theological beliefs, allowed me to lead, learn, and soar as a leader.

Regardless of your theology, being honest about the environment in which you are serving and leading, and discerning from the Lord what He is calling you to do, will help you know your next steps.

BEST PRACTICE #3: ENOUGH FOR EVERYONE MIND-SET

There is quite a bit of research about the "Queen Bee" syndrome. This shows up in work and leadership environments where a strong female leader rises in authority but views or treats other women poorly.[4] Queen bees haven't learned that God has room for everyone. For them there's an underlying fear that somehow leadership and influence are scarce, that there is a shortage of opportunity, or that if someone else succeeds, their chances of success somehow diminish. The Queen Bee syndrome can seep into all of us, often without us even noticing. And it tends to be cultivated in environments where female leaders are few or far between.

My friend, Amy, beautifully described her own wrestling with this mentality:

> I do think there is this one thing out there in this whole world of men and women called "gender bias" or "likability." And I could be wrong, but if I take a close look at myself, I have that. It's ironic because I'm a female in leadership. But I would give men the benefit of the doubt as they would lead or speak or teach. But with women, I kind of had this, "Prove it. Earn it with me" attitude. Somewhere along the line I was like, *This is ridiculous. Why would I have this view?*

My first step, honestly, was any time I saw, for example, a female teacher and those thoughts would come in, those "Prove it," or "We'll see if we like her" kind of thing, I would start praying for her. And God really started to change my heart that way. Because when you're praying for a female who's in front teaching or leading, and you're praying for her success, that starts to change your bias.

And then I started to realize, just in my own life probably as a mother and as a wife, how much women need women. And so, in those couple of years, I just changed altogether. And through my love and openness, that bias thinking I had really dissipated. But it was a very real thing for me.[5]

Growing an "Enough for Everyone" mind-set is critical in helping to free ourselves from self-imposed limitations, and being used by God to create healthier and more abundant environments for women leaders around us and those who will come after us.

Dee Ann Turner, vice president of sustainability, has spent the majority of her career developing and leading corporate talent at Chick-fil-A, Inc (CFA). As the first woman officer at her company and leading at the highest levels for more than thirty years, she has a unique and wise perspective on the power of a female leader's mind-set:

Unfortunately, I think sometimes when we have a difference like being female we have a scarcity mentality about opportunity. We think "There can only be *one* of this, or *one* of that," and certainly businesses and society have reinforced that in some ways. But what I prefer is an abundance mentality. That there's enough for everyone, so let's help everybody get there. Let's bring people along with us.

A friend of mine, named Lynn, and I both had that mentality. A lot of organizations end up having two female leaders and, for a long time, we were the only two female officers, and you would think we would have a lot of competition, but we just never allowed that. I mean, we were friends first, but even as our leadership developed, we just didn't allow it. As a matter of fact, Lynn was the person who led me to Africa for the first time. And we loved doing a lot of ministry work together outside of work.

One of the things that we found early on is that, because there were only two of us, there were a lot of women who wanted us to mentor them. Well, there just wasn't enough time to spend with all of them, so we came up with this idea. We were passionate about this work in Africa, and so we told this group of women, "Hey, here's the deal. We'll spend time with you every single month, if you'll participate in this program with us. So we did a twelve-month discipleship of these women where we spent time every month, and then we planned a project in Africa. Those women raised eighty thousand dollars to build a dining hall so the kids at the school didn't have to eat outside anymore. And then they planned a powerful program for ten secondary schools to minister to their teenage girls on prayer, purpose, and purity. It was so unbelievable.

In fact, some of their male supervisors were so impressed with what they were getting to do and the time we were investing in them, that they personally donated to the mission trip and then allowed them to take the time off as development time, because what they were learning was having such an impact on their business skills.

Lynn and I found ways to collaborate and synergize together instead of competing. Incidentally, Lynn became the first female member of CFA's executive committee and is now CFA's general counsel.[6]

Wow. Dee Ann's story demonstrates the power of making room in our hearts and lives to embrace other women, pray for them, invest in them, and celebrate their successes with them.

One of the challenges of being a misfit is that we often feel like we have to go it alone. But standing alone is not the same as being alone. There's room for everyone, including you. Reach out and make connections. If you keep running into "queen bees," keep looking until you find the rest of us misfits. We always have room for one more.

BEST PRACTICE #4: RARELY (IF EVER) PLAY CARDS

There are so many cards. There's the gender card, the God card, the mom card, the hormone card, the husband card, the "I'm more emotional" card, the victim card, the fear card, the theology card, the cramps card, and so on. They are so handy. Who can argue with them, right? Your kids need you. God told you. Your husband asked for it.

The problem with playing cards, however, is that they always backfire. If you play the "I'm more emotional" card because you responded disrespectfully in a meeting, you shouldn't then expect your leaders to give you high-profile assignments because you've shown them you can't be trusted to control your emotions.

One time I was mentoring several younger female leaders, and two of them brought their husbands to a meeting with their bosses. One was having trouble leaving the office on time because of the workload her boss was giving her. She brought her husband so he could explain to her boss that she needed to be able to prioritize their family and her boss had better let her leave on time. Her boss quickly agreed, but it also took her longer to learn how to delegate and grow in her leadership than was necessary. In my opinion, she shortchanged herself and limited her boss's ability to challenge and develop her.

The other brought her husband to meet with her bosses because she wasn't feeling valued or esteemed. She had expressed her strengths and desires for her calling to her bosses before, but hoped the authority of her husband would make them take her concerns more seriously. It didn't. And, unfortunately, her credibility as a humble and confident leader only diminished while her suspicions of gender bias increased. She didn't help herself at all.

If you are leading well, you know the responsibilities and priorities that you need to cover. If you need to set a boundary, then set a boundary. Don't try to explain why you need to leave, why you can't take on something extra, or blame something outside of yourself. They only discredit your ability to meet your responsibilities.

> Let your "Yes" be "Yes," and your "No," "No." For whatever is more than these is from the evil one. (Matt. 5:37 NKJV)

Leaders don't play cards. We lead well and we exercise "agency," which is the capacity to act independently and make our own choices. Granted, if your bosses want an explanation, certainly give it to them. And indeed, our personal lives affect what we do and the decisions we make. But too often women lead with excuses, rather than just leading.

My talented friend Kem talked about learning from her male coworker who had a special-needs son. He had to leave work at 3:30 p.m. every day to meet his son at the bus stop, because his wife also worked in the afternoons. He never played the kids card or the special-needs card. He never explained why he had to leave if a meeting was running late, he just said he had to go and then left. That was that. Most people knew why, but he didn't feel the need to explain it or justify it. He knew not to play cards.[7]

BEST PRACTICE #5: INVEST IN A SUPPORT SYSTEM

None of us can have it all, or at least not all at the same time. There are only so many hours in a day and so many things you can accomplish, no matter how well you've learned to lead. The good news is that you are a leader, and leaders know how to build and recruit a team. These are the top support systems that high-level female leaders invest in, regularly access, and have made the biggest difference in their life and leadership.

1. OUTSOURCE AS MUCH AS POSSIBLE

From housekeepers, to restaurants on Christmas Eve, to asking fellow school moms to buy double the back-to-school supplies, leaders figure out what they can easily delegate. Sometimes it's figuring out how to divvy out household responsibilities to our husband and kids, sometimes it's working with a teacher to get our child extra tutoring after school so we don't have to battle homework, or sometimes it's recruiting a family member to plan our child's birthday games.

The key is knowing what your best contribution is to the people you love and outsourcing as many of the other things as possible, and letting go of the guilt that you can't be everything to everyone. The goal is to just make sure the bases get covered by someone.

2. ASK FOR HELP

From husbands to kids to neighbors to church and family members, people want to help you! Men certainly have no problem asking for help, so why do we? We live in a unique time. There is no way we can do everything a full-time stay-at-home housewife did forty years ago, plus lead, work, or volunteer in a significant way. It's just not possible. We don't send our kids outside for hours on end unsupervised, and most of us don't live within walking distance of our parents or siblings to have an extra hand when we need it.

Our lives are complex and hard and disconnected. When we are feeling the strain or are maxed out on what we can accomplish on our own, we need to reassess, figure out what we can let go or hand off, and then ask for help. Sometimes the biggest help we might need is people praying for us. Several leaders I respect have recruited personal prayer teams they can reach out to for extra prayer support and ongoing encouragement in their calling.

For those who are married, many interviewees commented on what an incredible support their husbands are to them. Not just in personally supporting and encouraging them, but in practically carrying their fair share of the home and kids.

If you are struggling to get the support you need, make sure you figure out exactly what you need and ask clearly for it. Unfortunately, so far in our research, we have not identified any husbands who can read their wives' minds.

3. MIX UP YOUR MENTORS

Don't fall into a rut with mentors. According to the interviewees and survey results, some of the best mentoring came from men. Look for all sorts of people to learn from and model after, read broadly, listen to podcasts from different speakers and perspectives, and ask someone you admire if you can buy them coffee and then bring a list of thought-out questions.

Too often we want a deep, personal, long-lasting, and time-intensive relationship to feel properly "mentored." But this kind of relationship rarely happens, or at least not for very long. Give mentoring relationships room to breathe. Pursue learning, and God will bring the right people at the right time. And be ready, because they will likely come in unexpected packages.

4. NETWORK WITH PROFESSIONAL WOMEN FRIENDS

Relationship and connections are hard for female leaders, but it is especially hard when we lead in church and don't really have our church community to access, at least not at the same level of authenticity that we are used to. In addition, the dynamics of leading and being female are unique.

I've been so blessed to be a part of a network of women executive pastors for the last several years. The last time we were together, we accidentally nicknamed ourselves the "One-Eyed Unicorns." Plain unicorns were not quite unique enough for us, and we also only have one eye instead of two. We feel this unusual in the world!

One of the younger women in our group described it like this:

> I'm still trying to figure out what kind of support I need—I'm a weird woman. I'm a waffle, not spaghetti. What feeds other women doesn't feed me. I don't have a craving to go to the beach for the day. I love to shop, but I don't need to do that with a bunch of girlfriends. What do I need as a woman and as a leader? I think what I need is *identification*. Something that helps with the loneliness and isolation. Nothing is worse than going to a small group or ministry event with an expectation of connection and then turning into the pastor of the group.

Several women talked about building relationships or small groups with high-level Christian female leaders from the professional world, either within their church or through other networks. I remember what it was like when a well-known news anchorwoman at our church pursued a friendship with me as "a fellow woman with influence and power." I had no idea what a lifeline connecting with her would become.

Many talked about learning how they couldn't look to their work relationships to also be their closest friendships. And being that we usually had similar networks and probably knew some of the same people (but not always), our group became a safe place to build real friendships that weren't limited to just work and leadership, although those ended up being a big part of our conversations. We "did life together," and as our roles and seasons changed, our friendships had enough flexibility to stay intact, and we were able to support each other through those transitions.

One fellow woman executive pastor in our group recently said, "I'm not willing to accept the fact that what God has for everyone else He doesn't have for me." She went after high-capacity women in her church and formed her own small group with them. "They are my friends. We've served in Peru together. We know how to support one another." [8]

I think that's true for all of us. If God has community and connection and authentic friendships available for everyone else in our churches, then He has them for us as well.

These four ideas might not be the exact things you, your work, or your family need, but hopefully they will get you started on thinking through the kind of team and support systems you will need to joyfully and fruitfully fulfill all the callings God has given you.

WORDS OF ENCOURAGEMENT

At the end of every interview, I asked what she or he would say to an aspiring female ministry leader. Here is a collection of advice. May it inspire and challenge you in your next steps. We are cheering you on!

FROM YOUR FELLOW FEMALE LEADERS

- "Own it. Own your journey. Step up and put yourself in places that will develop you, sharpen you, and allow you to be seen."
- "The church needs you. The body of Christ needs you to be everything God created you to be. . . . This only works when everybody's doing everything God gave them to do."

- "It's not just about leadership development, it's about *spiritual leadership development*. When you are in spiritual leadership, which we are in the church, you are going to be attacked. Satan is not going to like what you're doing. And if you don't realize there is spiritual warfare out there, if you don't realize you have the tools through the Word of God to speak scripture into situations, and if you don't know you have to stay very close to God, you are going to be in trouble. Know in your heart who you are in God and know the tools that you have in Him so that you can succeed in spiritual leadership."

- "I would say tend to any chips on your shoulder—especially in seasons of anonymity. That's probably part of the purpose of that season in your life. Don't feel defective if there isn't a place for you yet."

- "I would say to her that you can be everything God has created and called you to be. I would say to her to walk in confidence in the fullness of that calling, knowing that God is with you. If you'll walk out the things He's given you to do He's going to empower you and He's going to help you."

- "Find a female leader who is further along. Maybe ask, 'Can I come over and get close and observe someone who is doing it well'?"

- "Stay *hungry* for leadership development. You are responsible for your own growth and development. Read all you can, especially when it pertains to growth and development."

- "Recognize the authority that is on your life is given by Christ alone and not by an organization or pastor or a title or position. Walking out what that authority looks like in life isn't about waiting for the opportunity. It's about allowing the Holy Spirit to guide you. Because there will be all these micro-opportunities along the way that you have to lean into and be faithful that will build your strength for leadership. I think sometimes we can overlook or downplay these micro-moments because we're waiting for the opportunity that looks like something."

- "Your authority is in who God created you to be. Nobody can add to or take that away from you. And the more sensitive you are to the Holy Spirit, the more you'll see those opportunities and walk in when the doors open. And do so with thankfulness."
- "Figure out where you find your value. All the other stuff is just ancillary."
- "Find a female who can coach and mentor you. But don't just look at what someone else can do to help you rise. Find someone who's younger than you whom you can pour into and take along on the journey with you. Find as many networks and places where you can plug in with women because you're working in a man's world. Take time to strengthen who you are as a person, and that probably is going to be in the context of other women."
- "Spend a lot of time learning the skills that you need and recognize the fact that you're probably going to have to do them better than the men."
- "You have got to get control of your emotions. You can't deny your emotions, but you can't drive from your emotions either. You have to drive from your calling, your training, and the abilities that God has given you."
- "When you feel like you have something to say or contribute, don't hold back. Say it!"
- "When you waste emotional and mental energy on something you really can't control, you're robbing yourself of all the other joys you could be having. At the end of the day, you need to tell yourself, 'I did the best I could.' You don't need to dedicate any energy to guilt."

- "If it's in your heart to do, find ways to do it, even if your title doesn't match."
- "God has uniquely created you as a female. There are parts of you that will tend to lead more out of emotion and a place of grace and compassion. That is needed in every corner and every sector of our world, not just in the church. Remember that people are the greatest gift that God gave us. And because we have this unique ability as women, sometimes we love deeper and see good in people that men don't always see. We need to lean into that."
- "Don't let being a female define your leadership. Let how God has gifted you define your leadership."
- "Just bring to the table what you have to bring to the table. Don't try to be a chameleon with your male counterparts. And don't be afraid to be confident in a role that has traditionally or primarily been a man's role. I love what Shelley Giglio said to a group of women I was with. 'If somebody told you that you don't have a seat at the table, it wasn't Jesus.' Be okay if there are things that you do or ways in which you are gifted that historically or traditionally have been set aside for men in the church."
- "Trust God. God controls the hearts of kings. He can do whatever he wants with whomever he wants. No one could keep me off the stage if that's where God wants me to be. Don't try to push yourself into it. If God called you, He's going to make a way."
- "It's not about fighting for an agenda. It's about serving the Lord and being wherever He wants you to serve. *Really* serving is all about servanthood. Be humble but do not be afraid to step in and lead with servanthood and humility—and *lead well*. You will be seen for who you are and what you have to bring."
- "Take a look at the church's leadership. Is this a leadership culture where women are allowed to use their gifts, talents, and passions? Start there."

- "Embrace feedback and find ways to minimize your blind spots."
- "You've got to do what you do out of obedience to how God has gifted you and what He's called you to do. But you have to do it under the authority you are under."
- "Be a great question asker—ask as many questions as possible and listen. Be grateful and communicate your gratitude before you ask for an opportunity. Don't step back and don't shy away. Go for it! Use your gifts. Fly, flourish, and honor along the way."
- "Fight those battles. Show up. We need your voice in our church. We need it in the kingdom. Look at the internal obstacles that may be are holding you back—those messages in your head that you're listening to. They're probably lies. Take those first steps as boldly as you can to walk through whatever door is open. Do the very best you can in those smaller arenas. God will notice, and other people will open new doors for you."

FROM THE GUYS

- "First, I would say I'm sorry that historically we have not made space for you. Lead, find your place, find your mentor, and serve. You can lead, serve, and influence without a title."
- "Make yourself available to God and make yourself available to your leaders. Just keep showing up, keep being there, and be ready to be used by God and your leaders. God will use you, but you've got to show up."
- "If you feel called to lead, you need to let your leaders know that you're sensing this call on your life and ask for their advice and counsel. Ask them to speak into areas that may be under-developed or that you need to work on. You may be a catalyst in helping to unlock something for other women."
- "Be ready to get uncomfortable because it's going to be. You

may have to work harder than others, but you'll be better for it. Your gifts and abilities will be stronger because you've pioneered a new expression of God's grace and leadership within your church."

- "As a leader, I'm not seeing anything in you that Jesus hasn't already seen. When Paul said you are God's handiwork and that you were created to do good works, there's no parameters on that—male or female. That's open to everybody."

- "To any young aspiring female leader in the church I would say, 'Soar!' Explore the spiritual gift of leadership. Explore your aptitude for it and let your learning and passion be unfettered. In this regard, the 'name it and claim it' idea is a pretty good one."

- "Learn from other male and female leaders. Find somebody, one or two people, who you can just periodically ask questions and grow and learn. I think that leadership development is really self-development at its core, so look for those opportunities that are going to just help you mature or develop in your leadership."

- "If you're in a place where you are just walking through mud because of the environment that you're in, make sure God has specifically called you there."

- "Lead to an 'Audience of One.' At the end of the day, our value as leaders will have to come from how we lead relative to what God is calling us to do."

- "Be the very best you can possibly be and look for the opportunities and the open doors. And when you have one, make the most of it. And if the door isn't open, you may need to give it a little push."

- "Be the best version of yourself. Don't try to be somebody else. Don't look at other great leaders and try to emulate the things that are not in sync with who you are. Be the best version of yourself. We don't need templates of other people showing up. What we need is *fully alive* women leaders in our churches."

AND FROM ME

One of the great honors of writing this book was being able to interview Nancy Beach, formerly of Willow Creek Community Church, author of *Gifted to Lead*, and, at least for me, one of my few female ministry role models who has been present since my early twenties. She has courageously and graciously been used by God at the forefront of raising gender issues in the evangelical church and is still helping to create safe and welcoming environments for women leaders.

I thought it would be appropriate to close with some of her thoughts on what it means to be one of the first to blaze a trail that other women will be able to follow.

> One of my shadow sides is that I care too much what people think of me. I manage my image and I seek approval. The combination of those shadows plus being the first woman to really be "out there," made me fear that I might mess up, either in my performance on the job, or morally, or in character, or in anything like that, and people would say, "Well, see, that's what happens when you put a woman in leadership." I was carrying a tremendous *weight*.
>
> Henry Gates is an African American professor at Harvard and he's on the board of many organizations where he's the only person of color. He calls it the "freight of being iconic," which is this weight of being a symbol for, in his case, race. And I think I've felt that freight of being iconic as representing my gender, which is ridiculous. I'm not representing all women, and nobody asked me to do that. But I knew that I was breaking new ground at my church and that other churches were watching. I just wanted to make sure I got it right.
>
> I look at some of the women who followed behind me, and I feel like I see some of the same tentativeness in them. I just want to say, "You know what? Go for it! We're all going to make mistakes. We are all so afraid to make mistakes but that is how we

learn. You just do the best you can with the knowledge you have. But you need to show up." It took me a while, but I have learned how to show up and have found my voice with greater strength.[9]

I told her she did get it right, and there are many of us receiving the benefits.

My prayer for you is that you would hear *God's* voice louder than anyone else's. When someone comments on your "nice birthing hips," forgets to include you in an opportunity, is afraid to work with you, overlooks you, dismisses your opinion, pays you less, or anything else that throws off your confidence or causes you to question your ability to be a force in the kingdom, I pray that you would hear God's voice reminding you of who you are, whose you are, and what really matters.

I believe that as long as we are faithful to keep showing up, keep leaning in to the sanctifying lessons God has for us, keep finding our voice, keep taking advantage of the doors God opens, and keep learning (even from our mistakes), we are doing our part. And the women after us will do their part. And we will see what happens when God unleashes the potential of His *women* in His kingdom.

I cannot wait to see it.

To God be the glory.

BEST PRACTICES FOR FEMALE LEADERS DISCUSSION QUESTIONS

1. What has been the hardest part of getting clear on your calling?
2. How well do you know and understand your ministry environment?
3. On a scale of 1 to 10 (with 10 being the most natural), how

natural is it for you to have an "Enough for Everyone" mind-set?

4. What cards are you mostly likely to play? How can you approach difficult situations in a healthy but assertive way?

5. Do you have support systems? If so, how often do you invest in or access them? What is one thing you can do this week to be more involved?

6. Which statement from the "Words of Encouragement" section spoke to you the most, and why?

ACKNOWLEDGMENTS

'd like to thank the countless men and women who work hard every day to help others grow and develop, especially in the local church. I am a recipient of your passion and gifts. May we all be faithful to pass along the greatest gift of all, faith in Jesus, and what it takes to lead well in challenging times.

This project would not be possible without the generosity of the incredible people I had the privilege to interview and the more than one thousand female leaders around the globe who graciously shared their stories and perspectives in our survey. Thank you for showing up, letting your voices be heard, and sharing your stories with all of us.

Thank you to Amber Smart, Amy Anderson, Andrea Lathrop, Ashley Murphy, Becca Rowe, Bill Willits, Crystal Hart, Danielle Best, Debbie Pell, Dee Ann Turner, Denise McCleese, Giselle Jenkins, Heather Magnum, Janet McMahan, Jeanne Stevens, Jenni Catron, Jerry Hurley, Jo Anne Lyon, John Ortberg, Jon Ferguson, Judy West, Julie Bullock, Kathy Beechum, Kem Meyer, Kristi Kirschmann, Lindsay Willis, Mallory Bassham, Nancy Beach, Renee Cole, Sherry Surratt, Todd Mullins, and the women of the 2018 Women Executive Pastors' Group Gathering.

A big thank you to the Kadi Cole & Company team for your belief in me and those we are called to serve. Special thanks to Renée Miller and Danielle Borzillo, for all your incredible work behind the scenes. And an especially big thank you to Carolyn Reed Master, for your expertise, encouragement, and incredibly hard work getting this book ready for the publisher. I could not have done this without you. Our almost twenty-year friendship is a treasure.

To the teams at Thomas Nelson/HarperCollins Christian Publishing and Leadership Network, especially Joey Paul and Greg Ligon: thank you for courageously taking a risk on me and this topic. A special thank-you to Susan Ligon for your friendship and professional investment in me.

Thank you to . . .

My friends, who unwaveringly supported this project and gave me critical and much-needed feedback on all stages of the concepts and manuscript: I love and appreciate each of you.

My fellow one-eyed unicorns of the Women Executive Pastors' Group: I am so glad we get to be misfits together.

Judy West, for your friendship, incredible mind, and countless hours of wise feedback.

Debbie Pell and Jeannette Cochran, for your passion and gift of helping me think bigger.

Jill Brandenburg: This book feels like yet another extension of your leadership in my life. Thank you for everything.

My mom, for being my trusted first round of feedback and always cheering me on, even if you weren't quite sure what I was talking about.

Karen McNenny: You are my lifelong friend, professional colleague, abundance mentor, and personal cheerleader. McLangy always.

My personal sisterhood, who support, encourage, and pray for me—Robin Stark, Sara Grace Wall, Renee Cole, Wendy Colbo, Renee

Travis, Sue Muller, Bev Bonner, Brenda Sue Cole, Sandy Crawford, and in memory of Heather Koller: you are each such a treasure in my life.

My awesome family, Matt and Ethan: Thank you for not only supporting me, but never complaining as I work. I love you so much. You are the most important of all my callings.

And a final thank-you to our magnificent Lord. What an adventure it is to love and follow You. I wouldn't trade it for anything.

NOTES

WELCOME

1. Vivian Hunt, Dennis Layton, and Sara Prince, *Diversity Matters* (McKinsey & Company; February 2, 2015), https://www.mckinsey .com/~/media/mckinsey/business%20functions/organization /our%20insights/why%20diversity%20matters/diversity%20matters .ashx.

BEST PRACTICE #1: SEEK TO UNDERSTAND

1. Leadership Network (http://leadnet.org/) is a leadership collaborative for pastors and churches with more than two hundred thousand church leaders around the world engaging in the network to acquire innovative knowledge and drive local ministry impact.

2. David M. Scholer, "1 Timothy 2:9–15 & the Place of Women in the Church's Ministry," in *Women, Authority & The Bible*, ed. Alvera Michelsen (Downers Grove, IL: InterVarsity Press, 1986), 193–219.

3. Robyn Wilkerson, *Shattering the Stained Glass Ceiling: A Coaching Strategy for Women Leaders in Ministry* (Springfield, MO: Influence Resources, 2017), 5.

4. U.S. Const. amend. XIX.

5. Equal Pay Act of 1963 (EPA), 29 U.S.C. Chapter 8, § 206(d).

6. Equal Credit Opportunity Act, 12 USC 1691 et seq. (1975 L).

7. Taylor v. Louisiana, 419 U.S. 522 (1975).

8. Pub. L. No. 95-555, 92 Stat. 2076 (1978).

9. 42 U.S. Code § 2000e_4, Equal Employment Opportunity Commission.

10. Julie Roys, host, "What Is God's Vision for Womanhood?" *Up for Debate* (MP3 podcast), Moody Bible Radio, December 9, 2017, https://moodyaudio.com/products/what-gods-vision-womanhood.

11. Danielle Best, interview by Kadi Cole, Royal Palm Beach, Florida, February 14, 2018.

12. J J DiGeronimo, "Sticky Floor Syndrome and Other Self Sabotage," https://www.jjdigeronimo.com/sticky-floor-syndrome-self-sabotage/, JJ DiGeronimo's website, accessed April 16, 2018.

13. Rebecca Shambaugh, *It's Not a Glass Ceiling, It's a Sticky Floor: Free Yourself from the Hidden Behaviors Sabotaging Your Career Success* (New York: McGraw-Hill, 2008), xiii–xv.

14. Tara Mohair, "Why Women Don't Apply for Jobs Unless They're 100% Qualified," *Harvard Business Review*, August 24, 2014, https://hbr.org/2014/08/why-women-dont-apply-for-jobs-unless-theyre-100-qualified.

15. DiGeronimo, "Sticky Floor Syndrome and Other Self Sabotage."

BEST PRACTICE #2: CLEARLY DEFINE WHAT YOU BELIEVE

1. Bill Willits, interview by Kadi Cole, Royal Palm Beach, FL, February 22, 2018.

2. Female Church Leaders Survey, February 2018, https://www.surveymonkey.com/r/FemaleChurchLeadersSurvey.

3. Female Church Leaders Survey.

4. Marco Antonio de Dominis, *De Republica Ecclesiastica* (London: Billius, 1617), 1:676.

5. Wayne Grudem, *Systematic Theology: An Introduction to Biblical Doctrine* (Grand Rapids, MI: Zondervan, 1994), 244.

6. Charles Ryrie, *Basic Theology* (Wheaton, IL: Victor Books, 1986), 57–58.

7. Kevin Giles, *The Trinity & Subordinationism: The Doctrine of God & the Contemporary Gender Debate* (Downers Grove, IL: IVP Academic, 2002), 15.

8. Dictionary.com, http://www.dictionary.com/browse/equalitarianism.

9. Grudem, *Systematic Theology*, 245.

10. For further study on the biblical and theological positions of egalitarianism and complementarianism, please consider consulting the following sources: CBE International (Christians for Biblical Equality), https://www.cbeinternational.org/; CBMW (the Council on Biblical Manhood and Womanhood), https://cbmw.org.

11. The content on Adrian Warnock's blog post was used in the creation of the theological chart. See Warnock, "Gender: Complementarian vs Egalitarian Spectrum," September 24, 2012, http://www.patheos.com/blogs/adrianwarnock/2012/09/gender-roles-a-complementarian-and-egalitarian-spectrum/.

12. 61 percent stat: U.S. Congregations, Blog, February 2, 2017, accessed February 16, 2018, http://www.uscongregations.org/blog/2014/02/17/what-are-the-major-challenges-that-u-s-congregations-face/.

BEST PRACTICE #3: MINE THE MARKETPLACE

1. Kathy Beechum, interview by Kadi Cole, Royal Palm Beach, FL, January 20, 2018.

2. Robin J. Ely, Herminina Ibarra, and Deborah Kolb, "Taking Gender into Account: Theory and Design for Women's Leadership Development Programs," *Academy of Management Learning & Education* 10, no. 3 (September 2011): 3, https://www.hbs.edu/faculty/Pages/item.aspx?num=41610.

3. Andrea Lathrop, interview by Kadi Cole, Royal Palm Beach, FL, January 24, 2018.

4. James Strong, *The Strongest Strong's Exhaustive Concordance of the Bible* (Grand Rapids, MI: Zondervan, 2001), 1623.

5. Jenny Catron, interviewed by Kadi Cole, Royal Palm Beach, January 16, 2018.

6. Mallory Basham, WXP Breakfast meeting at XP Conference at Gateway Church in Southlake, Texas, with Kadi Cole, March 8, 2018.

7. Efrem Smith, et al., *Let Women Lead*, Missio Alliance, February 22 2018, Live Webinar, https://www.missioalliance.org/product/let-women-lead-webinar/.

8. Women's Executive Pastor roundtable discussion, Dallas, Texas, March 8, 2018.

9. Barna Group, "Christian Women Today, Part 1 of 4: What Women Think of Faith, Leadership and Their Role in the Church," Barna. com, August 13, 2012, https://www.barna.com/research /christian-women-today-part-1-of-4-what-women-think-of-faith -leadership-and-their-role-in-the-church/.

10. Linda Schantz, Women's Executive Pastor breakfast discussion with Kadi Cole, Dallas, Texas, March 8, 2018.

11. Ashley Murphy, interview by Kadi Cole, Royal Palm Beach, FL, February 1, 2018.

12. Jerry Hurley, interview by Kadi Cole, Royal Palm Beach, FL, February 15, 2018.

13. Stephen J. Dubner, "After a Glass Ceiling; A Glass Cliff," *Freakonomics Podcast*, February 14, 2018, http://freakonomics.com/podcast/glass -cliff/.

BEST PRACTICE #4: INTEGRATE SPIRITUAL FORMATION AND LEADERSHIP DEVELOPMENT

1. Rod Rogers, *Pastor Driven Stewardship: 10 Steps to Lead Your Church to Biblical Giving* (Dallas, TX: Brown Books, 2006), 92.

2. Jeanne Stevens, interview by Kadi Cole, Royal Palm Beach, FL, April 19, 2018.

3. Andrea Lathrop, interview by Kadi Cole, Royal Palm Beach, FL, January 24, 2018.

4. *Female Church Leaders Survey*, (see chap. 2, n. 3).

5. U.S. Congregations, "What Are the Major Challenges That U.S. Congregations Face?," *USCLS* (U.S. Congregational Life Survey blog), accessed October 10, 2018, http://www.uscongregations.org/blog/ 2014/02/17/what-are-the-major-challenges-that-u-s-congregations -face/.

6. Jill Brandenburg, interview by Kadi Cole, Royal Palm Beach, FL, January 23, 2018.

7. Dr. J. Robert Clinton, *The Making of a Leader: Recognizing the Lessons*

and Stages of Leadership Development (Colorado Springs: NavPress, 2012), 22.

8. Catalyst, "Damned or Doomed: Catalyst Study on Gender Stereotyping at Work Uncovers Double-Bind Dilemmas for Women," Catalyst.org, http://www.catalyst.org/media/damned-or-doomed -catalyst-study-gender-stereotyping-work-uncovers-double-bind -dilemmas-women (accessed March 14, 2018).

9. Sheryl Sandberg, *Lean In: Women, Work and the Will to Lead* (New York: Alfred A. Knopf, 2013), 39–40.

10. Kathleen L. McGinn and Nicole Tempest, "Heidi Roizen," Harvard Business School Case 800-228, January 2000 (revised April 2010), https://www.hbs.edu/faculty/Pages/item.aspx?num=26880.

11. Becca Rowe, interview by Kadi Cole, Royal Palm Beach, FL, February 1, 2018.

12. Judy West, interview by Kadi Cole, Royal Palm Beach, FL, January 16, 2018.

13. Jo Anne Lyon, interview by Kadi Cole, Royal Palm Beach, FL, January 23, 2018.

14. *Female Church Leaders Survey.*

15. Amy Anderson, interview by Kadi Cole, Royal Palm Beach, FL, January 17, 2018.

16. Pauline Rose Clance and Suzanne Imes, "The Imposter Phenomenon in High Achieving Women: Dynamics and Therapeutic Intervention," *Psychotherapy Theory, Research and Practice* 15, no 3 (fall 1978): 1, http://www.paulineroseclance.com/pdf/ip_high _achieving_women.pdf.

17. Amber Smart, interview by Kadi Cole, Royal Palm Beach, FL, January 15, 2018.

18. Steven J. Stein and Howard E. Book, *The EQ Edge: Emotional Intelligence and Your Success* (Mississauga, ON: Jossey-Bass, 2006), 13–26.

19. Debbie Pell, interview by Kadi Cole, Royal Palm Beach, FL, January 17, 2018.

20. John M. Grohol, "15 Cognitive Distortions," Psych Central, updated,

April 12, 2018, https://psychcentral.com/lib/15-common-cognitive
-distortions/.

21. Reuven Bar-On, "The BarOn Model of Social and Emotional
    Intelligence (ESI)," *Psicothema* 18 Suppl (February 2006): S 13–25,
    http://www.eiconsortium.org/reprints/bar-on_model_of
    _emotional-social_intelligence.htm.

22. Henry Cloud and John Townsend, *How People Grow: What the Bible
    Reveals About Personal Growth* (Grand Rapids, MI: Zondervan, 1996), 117.

23. Bob Goff, *Everybody Always* (Nashville: Nelson Books, 2018), 165.

24. Carolyn Cunningham, "Gender Differences in Communication
    and How That Impacts Women's Advancement," Women Lead
    Conference, Spokane, WA, March 14, 2018.

25. Debbie Pell, interview by Kadi Cole, Royal Palm Beach, FL, January
    17, 2018.

26. Cunningham, "Gender Differences in Communication."

27. Peter Scazzero, *The Emotionally Healthy Leader: How Transforming
    Your Inner Life Will Deeply Transform Your Church, Team, and the World*
    (Grand Rapids: Zondervan, 2015), 50.

28. Kem Meyer, interviewed by Kadi Cole, Royal Palm Beach, FL,
    February 7, 2018.

29. Parker Palmer, *Let Your Life Speak: Listening for the Voice of Your
    Vocation* (San Francisco: Jossey-Bass, 2000), 78.

30. Cloud and Townsend, *How People Grow*, 134.

BEST PRACTICE #5: BE AN "OTHER"

1. Henry Cloud, *The Power of the Other: The Startling Effect Other People
   Have on You, from the Boardroom to the Bedroom and Beyond—and What
   to Do About It* (New York: Harper, 2016), 8–9.

2. Cloud, 13.

3. Sherry Surratt, interview by Kadi Cole, Royal Palm Beach, FL,
   January 29, 2018.

4. *Female Church Leaders Survey* (see chap. 2, n. 3).

5. Dan Schawbel, "Sylvia Ann Hewlett: Find a Sponsor Instead of a
   Mentor," *Forbes*, September 10, 2013, https://www.forbes.com/sites

/danschawbel/2013/09/10/sylvia-ann-hewlett-find-a-sponsor-instead
-of-a-mentor/2/#41aa5359330b.

6. *Female Church Leaders Survey.*

7. Gail M. McGuire, "Gender, Race, and the Shadow Structure: A Study
of Informal Networks and Inequality in a Work Organization,"
Gender and Society 16, no. 3 (2002): 303–22, http://www.jstor.org
/stable/3081781.

8. *Female Church Leaders Survey.*

9. Anna Marie Valerio and Kartina Sawyer, "The Men Who Mentor
Women," *Harvard Business Review*, December 7, 2016, https://hbr.org
/2016/12/the-men-who-mentor-women.

10. Valerio and Sawyer.

11. Susan Colantuono, "The Career Advice You Probably Didn't Get,"
TED, November 16, 2013, https://www.ted.com/talks/susan
_colantuono_the_career_advice_you_probably_didn_t_get.

12. Sylvia Ann Hewlett, *Forget a Mentor, Find a Sponsor* (Boston, MA:
Harvard Business Review Press, 2013), 18–20, Kindle.

13. Jennifer Ludden, "Ask for a Raise? Most Women Hesitate," NPR,
February 8, 2011, https://www.npr.org/2011/02/14/133599768
/ask-for-a-raise-most-women-hesitate.

14. Dan Schawbel, "Sylvia Ann Hewlett: Find a Sponsor Instead of a
Mentor," *Forbes*, September 10, 2013, https://www.forbes.com/sites
/danschawbel/2013/09/10/sylvia-ann-hewlett-find-a-sponsor-instead
-of-a-mentor/2/#41aa5359330b.

15. Schawbel.

16. Jerry Hurley, interview by Kadi Cole, Royal Palm Beach, FL,
February 15, 2018.

17. Carolyn Gordon, in "Women in Ministry," YouTube video, 1:51,
posted by Fuller Theological Seminary, August 19, 2015, https://
www.youtube.com/watch?v=D-GqCCmJIAs.

18. Bill Willits, interview by Kadi Cole, Royal Palm Beach, FL, February
22, 2018.

19. Arlie Hochschild, with Anne Machung, *The Second Shift: Working
Families and the Revolution at Home* (New York: Penguin Group, 2012), 4.

20. Sylvia Ann Hewlett, *Executive Presence: The Missing Link Between Merit and Success* (New York: HarperCollins, 2014), 166.

21. Judy West, interview by Kadi Cole, Royal Palm Beach, FL, January 22, 2018.

BEST PRACTICE #6: CREATE AN ENVIRONMENT OF SAFETY

1. Laura Santhanam, "Poll: A Third of Women Say They've Been Sexually Harassed or Abused at Work," PBS News Hour, November 21, 2017, https://www.pbs.org/newshour/nation /poll-a-third-of-women-say-theyve-been-sexually-harassed-or -abused-at-work.

2. *Female Church Leaders Survey* (see chap. 2, n. 3).

3. Claire Miller, "Unintended Consequences of Sexual Harassment Scandals," *New York Times*, October 9, 2017, https://www.nytimes .com/2017/10/09/upshot/as-sexual-harassment-scandals-spook-men -it-can-backfire-for-women.html (accessed April 20, 2018).

4. Billy Graham, *Just As I Am* (New York: HarperCollins, 1997), 128–29.

5. Joseph Myers, *The Search to Belong: Rethinking Intimacy, Community, and Small Groups* (Grand Rapids: Zondervan, 2003), 20, 39–54.

6. Karen Longman, "Sticky Floors? Stained Glass Ceilings? Addressing Barriers That Deter Women from Leadership," Breakout Sessions, Advancing Women in Leadership Conference, Azusa, CA, March 5, 2018.

7. Peggy Martin, *The Therapeutic Use of Self* (London: Palgrave, 1987), 38.

8. L. Gunzareth, V., et al., "National Institute on Alcohol Abuse and Alcoholism Report on Moderate Drinking," Alcohol: Clinical and Experimental Research 28, no. 6 (June 2004): 829–47, https://www .ncbi.nlm.nih.gov/pubmed/15201626.

9. John Ortberg, email interview by Kadi Cole, February 8, 2018.

10. *Female Church Leaders Survey.*

11. "Harassment," US Equal Employment Opportunity Commission, accessed May 2, 2018, https://www.eeoc.gov/laws/types/harassment .cfm.

BEST PRACTICE #7: UPGRADE YOUR PEOPLE PRACTICES

1. Kem Meyer (see chap. 4, n. 28).
2. Keith Payne, Laura Niemi, and John M. Doris, "How to Think About 'Implicit Bias,'" *Scientific American*, March 27, 2018, https://www.scientificamerican.com/article/how-to-think-about-implicit-bias/.
3. Emily Pronin, Daniel Y. Lin, and Lee Ross, "The Bias Blind Spot: Perceptions of Bias in Self Versus Others," Personality and Social Psychology Bulletin 28, no. 3 (March 2002): 369–81, https://doi.org/10.1177/0146167202286008.
4. Kate Shellnut, "Women's March Sets Out to Exclude 40 Percent of American Women," *Christianity Today*, January 18, 2017, https://www.christianitytoday.com/women/2017/january/womens-march-sets-out-to-exclude-40-percent-of-american-wom.html.
5. Laura Ortberg Turner, "The Christian F-Word," *Christianity Today*, September 25, 2013, https://www.christianitytoday.com/women/2013/september/christian-f-word.html.
6. Max de Pree, *Leadership Is an Art* (New York: Random House, 2004), 11.
7. *Female Church Leaders Survey* (see chap. 2, n. 3).
8. Kathryn Vasel, "5 Things to Know About the Gender Pay Gap," CNN Money, April 4, 2017, http://money.cnn.com/2017/04/04/pf/equal-pay-day-gender-pay-gap/index.html?iid=EL.
9. Ashley Milne-Tyte, host, Episode 105: "The Assistant," The Broad Experience (MP3 podcast), May 15, 2017, https://itunes.apple.com/us/podcast/the-broad-experience/id524835071?mt=2.
10. Julia Carpenter, "Why Men Need to Believe in the Wage Gap," CNN Business, February 20, 2018, http://money.cnn.com/2018/02/20/pf/men-wage-gap/index.html.
11. Cyrus Schleifer and Amy D Miller, "Occupational Gender Inequality Among American Clergy, 1976–2016: Revisiting the Stained-Glass Ceiling," *Sociology of Religion* 78, no. 4 (January 8, 2018): 387–410, https://doi.org/10.1093/socrel/srx032.
12. *Female Church Leaders Survey* (see chap. 2, n. 3).
13. *Female Church Leaders Survey*.
14. *Female Church Leaders Survey*.

15. *Female Church Leaders Survey.*

16. Shelley Correll, Stephan Benard, and In Paik, "Getting a Job: Is There a Motherhood Penalty?" Harvard Kennedy School Women and Public Policy Program, Gender Action Portal, March 2007, http://gap.hks.harvard.edu/getting-job-there-motherhood-penalty (accessed April 25, 2018).

17. *Female Church Leaders Survey.*

18. The Sloan Center on Aging & Work at Boston College, "Workers Need: Improved Performance & Productivity," http://workplaceflexibility.bc.edu/need/need_employers_performance (accessed May 25, 2018).

19. Jerry Hurley, interview by Kadi Cole, Royal Palm Beach, FL, February 15, 2018.

20. Kem Meyer, interview by Kadi Cole, Royal Palm Beach, FL, February 7, 2018.

21. Shelley Correll and Caroline Simard, "Research: Vague Feedback Is Holding Women Back," *Harvard Business Review*, April 29, 2016, https://hbr.org/2016/04/research-vague-feedback-is-holding-women-back.

22. Paola Cecchi-Dimeglio, "How Gender Bias Corrupts Performance Reviews and What to Do About It," *Harvard Business Review*, April 12, 2017, https://hbr.org/2017/04/how-gender-bias-corrupts-performance-reviews-and-what-to-do-about-it.

23. Jack Warren and Cindy Park, interview by Kadi Cole, Royal Palm Beach, FL, April 24, 2018.

24. *Female Church Leaders Survey.*

25. *Female Church Leaders Survey.*

26. *Female Church Leaders Survey.*

27. *Female Church Leaders Survey.*

28. *Female Church Leaders Survey.*

29. *Female Church Leaders Survey.*

BEST PRACTICE #8: TAKE ON YOUR CULTURE

1. David Campbell, David Edgar, and George Stonehouse, *Business Strategy: An Introduction*, 3rd ed. (London: Palgrave Macmillan, 2011), 263.

2. Wikipedia, s.v. "ecotone," last modified September 8, 2018, https://en.wikipedia.org/wiki/Ecotone.

3. Susan Walker, et al., "Properties of Ecotones: Evidence from Five Ecotones Objectively Determined from a Coastal Vegetation Gradient," *Journal of Vegetation Science* 14, no. 4 (April 9, 2009): 579–90, https://doi.org/10.1111/j.1654-1103.2003.tb02185.x.

4. Ken Behr, "How Christian Subculture Can Be a Stumbling Block," *Church Executive* (blog), June 7, 2012, https://churchexecutive.com/archives/how-christian-subculture-can-be-a-stumbling-block.

5. Behr.

6. Carolyn Cunningham, "Gender Differences in Communications and How That Impacts Women's Advancement," Women Lead Conference, Spokane, WA, March 14, 2018.

7. Lindsay Willis, interview by Kadi Cole, Royal Palm Beach, FL, January 24, 2018.

8. Susan Chira, "The Universal Phenomenon of Men Interrupting Women," *New York Times*, June 14, 2017, https://www.nytimes.com/2017/06/14/business/women-sexism-work-huffington-kamala-harris.html.

9. Jessica Bennett, "How Not to Be 'Manterrupted' in Meetings," *Time*, January 20, 2015, http://time.com/3666135/sheryl-sandberg-talking-while-female-manterruptions/.

10. Henry Louis Mencken, *Prejudices: Second Series* (New York: Alfred A. Knopf, 1920), 155.

11. Joan C. Williams, "What Works for Women at Work," video, Stanford VMware Women's Leadership Innovation Lab, accessed October 11, 2018, https://womensleadership.stanford.edu/whatworks.

12. Tony Hsieh, *Delivering Happiness: A Path to Profits, Passion, and Purpose* (New York: Business Plus, 2010), 154.

13. Janet H. Cho, "'Diversity Is Being Asked to the Party; Inclusion Is Being Asked to Dance' Verna Myers Tells Cleveland Bar," Cleveland.com, May 27, 2016, http://www.cleveland.com/business/index.ssf/2016/05/diversity_is_being_invited_to.html.

14. Ann Sweigart, "Women on Board for Change: The Norway Model of Boardroom Quotas as a Tool for Progress in the United States and Canada," *Northwest Journal of International Law & Business* 32, no. 4 (2012): 81A, http://scholarlycommons.law.northwestern.edu/njilb /vol32/iss4/6.

15. Belle Derks et al., "Do Sexist Organizational Cultures Create the Queen Bee?" *British Journal of Social Psychology* 50, no. 3 (September 2011): 519–35, https://doi.org/10.1348/014466610X525280.

16. Jon Ferguson, interview by Kadi Cole, Royal Palm Beach, FL, January 15, 2018.

17. Ferguson.

NEXT STEPS AND FINAL THOUGHTS FOR CHURCHES

1. Krissah Thompson, "In March on Washington, White Activists Were Largely Overlooked but Strategically Essential," *Washington Post*, August 25, 2013, https://www.washingtonpost.com/lifestyle/style /in-march-on-washington-white-activists-were-largely-overlooked -but-strategically-essential/2013/08/25/f2738c2a-eb27-11e2-8023 -b7f07811d98e_story.html?utm_term=.d975b97a5a9c.

2. Barna Group, "Christian Women Today, Part 1 of 4: What Women Think of Faith, Leadership and Their Role in the Church," Barna, August 13, 2012, https://www.barna.com/research/christian-women -today-part-1-of-4-what-women-think-of-faith-leadership-and-their -role-in-the-church/.

3. Jo Anne Lyon, interview by Kadi Cole, Royal Palm Beach, FL, January 23, 2018.

BEST PRACTICES FOR FEMALE LEADERS

1. The Holiday, directed by Nancy Meyer, Columbia Pictures, 2006.

2. Phil-Israel, *The Banner of Israel* vol. 17 (2012), 482, www. RareBooksClub.com.

3. Phil-Israel, *The Banner of Israel.*

4. Belle Derks, Naomi Ellemers, Colette van Laar, and Kim de Groot, "Do Sexist Organizational Cultures Create the Queen Bee?" *British*

Journal of Social Psychology (2010), accessed May 26, 2018, https://onlinelibrary.wiley.com/doi/pdf/10.1348/014466610X525280.

5. Amy Anderson, interview by Kadi Cole, Royal Palm Beach, FL, January 17, 2018.

6. Dee Ann Turner, interview by Kadi Cole, Royal Palm Beach, FL, February 1, 2018.

7. Kem Meyer, interview by Kadi Cole, Royal Palm Beach, FL, February 7, 2018.

8. Women's Executive Pastor Roundtable Discussion, Dallas, TX, March 8, 2018.

9. Nancy Beach, interview by Kadi Cole, Royal Palm Beach, FL, January 16, 2018.

BIBLIOGRAPHY

Barna Group, Inc. "Christian Women Today, Part 1 of 4: What Women Think of Faith, Leadership and Their Role in the Church." Barna. August 13, 2012. https://www.barna.com/research/christian-women -today-part-1-of-4-what-women-think-of-faith-leadership-and-their -role-in-the-church/.

Behr, Ken. "How Christian Subculture Can Be a Stumbling Block." *Church Executive* (blog). Posted June 7, 2012. https://churchexecutive.com /archives/how-christian-subculture-can-be-a-stumbling-block.

Bennett, Jessica. "How Not to Be 'Manterrupted' in Meetings." *Time.* January 20, 2015. http://time.com/3666135/sheryl-sandberg-talking -while-female-manterruptions/.

Campbell, David, David Edgar, and George Stonehouse. *Business Strategy: An Introduction*, 3rd ed. London: Palgrave Macmillan, 2011.

Carpenter, Julia. "Why Men Need to Believe in the Wage Gap." CNN Business. February 20, 2018. http://money.cnn.com/2018/02/20/pf /men-wage-gap/index.html.

Catalyst. "Damned or Doomed—Catalyst Study on Gender Stereotyping at Work Uncovers Double-Bind Dilemmas for Women." http://www .catalyst.org/media/damned-or-doomed-catalyst-study-gender -stereotyping-work-uncovers-double-bind-dilemmas-women.

Cecchi-Dimeglio, Paola. "How Gender Bias Corrupts Performance Reviews and What to Do About It." *Harvard Business Review.* April 12, 2017. https://hbr.org/2017/04/how-gender-bias-corrupts-performance -reviews-and-what-to-do-about-it.

Chira, Susan. "The Universal Phenomenon of Men Interrupting Women." *New York Times.* June 14, 2017. https://www.nytimes.com/2017/06/14 /business/women-sexism-work-huffington-kamala-harris.html.

Cho, Janet H. "'Diversity Is Being Asked to the Party; Inclusion Is Being Asked to Dance' Verna Myers Tells Cleveland Bar." Cleveland.com. May 27, 2016. http://www.cleveland.com/business/index.ssf/2016/05 /diversity_is_being_invited_to.htm.

Clance, Pauline Rose, and Suzanne Imes. "The Imposter Phenomenon in High Achieving Women: Dynamics and Therapeutic Intervention." *Psychotherapy Theory, Research and Practice* 15, no. 3 (fall 1978): 1. http:// www.paulineroseclance.com/pdf/ip_high_achieving_women.pdf.

Clinton, J. Robert. *The Making of a Leader: Recognizing the Lessons and Stages of Leadership Development.* Colorado Springs, CO: NavPress, 2012.

Cloud, Henry, and John Townsend. *How People Grow: What the Bible Reveals about Personal Growth.* Orange, FL: Zondervan, 1996.

———. *The Power of the Other: The Startling Effect Other People Have on You, from the Boardroom to the Bedroom and Beyond—and What to Do About It.* New York: Harper, 2016.

Colantuono, Susan. "The Career Advice You Probably Didn't Get." TED, November 16, 2013. https://www.ted.com/talks/susan_colantuono _the_career_advice_you_probably_didn_t_get.

Correll, Shelley, and Caroline Simard. "Research: Vague Feedback Is Holding Women Back." *Harvard Business Review.* April 29, 2016. https://hbr.org/2016/04/research-vague-feedback-is-holding-women -back.

Correll, Shelley, Stephan Benard, and In Paik. "Getting a Job: Is There a Motherhood Penalty?" Harvard Kennedy School Women and Public Policy Program, Gender Action Portal. March 2007. http://gap. hks.harvard.edu/getting-job-there-motherhood-penalty. Accessed April 25, 2018.

Cunningham, Carolyn. "Gender Differences in Communication and How That Impacts Women's Advancement." Women Lead Conference. Spokane, Washington. March 14, 2018.

de Dominis, Marco Antonio. *De Republica Ecclesiastica*. Vol. 1. London: Billius, 1617.

de Pree, Max. *Leadership Is an Art*. New York: Random House, 2004.

Derks, Belle, Naomi Ellemers, Colette van Laar, and Kim de Groot. "Do Sexist Organizational Cultures Create the Queen Bee?" *British Journal of Social Psychology* 50, no. 3 (September 2011). https://doi.org /10.1348/014466610X525280.

DiGeronimo, J J. "Sticky Floor Syndrome and Other Self Sabotage." *J J DiGeronimo* (blog). https://www.jjdigeronimo.com/sticky-floor -syndrome-self-sabotage/. Accessed April 16, 2018.

Dubner, Stephen J. "After a Glass Ceiling; A Glass Cliff." *Freakonomics Podcast*. Posted on February 14, 2018. http://freakonomics.com /podcast/glass-cliff/. Accessed March 22, 2018.

Ely, Robin J., Herminina Ibarra, and Deborah Kolb. "Taking Gender into Account: Theory and Design for Women's Leadership Development Programs." *Academy of Management Learning & Education*, 10 no. 3 (September 2011): 3. https://www.hbs.edu/faculty/Pages/item.aspx ?num=41610.

Giles, Kevin. *The Trinity & Subordinationism: The Doctrine of God & the Contemporary Gender Debate*. Downers Grove, IL: IVP Academic, 2002.

Goff, Bob. *Everybody Always*. Nashville, TN: Nelson Books, 2018.

Gordon, Carolyn. "Women in Ministry." Fuller Theological Seminary. Posted August 19, 2015. https://youtu.be/D-GqCCmJIAs.

Graham, Billy. *Just As I Am*. New York: HarperCollins, 1997.

Grohol, John M. "15 Common Cognitive Distortions." Psych Central. Last updated April 12, 2018. https://psychcentral.com/lib/15-common -cognitive-distortions/. Accessed May 29, 2018.

Grudem, Wayne. *Systematic Theology: An Introduction to Biblical Doctrine*. Grand Rapids, MI: Zondervan, 1994.

Gunzareth, L., V. Faden, S. Zakhari, and K. Warren. "National Institute on Alcohol Abuse and Alcoholism Report on Moderate Drinking."

Alcohol: Clinical and Experimental Research 28, no. 6 (June 2004): 829–47. https://www.ncbi.nlm.nih.gov/pubmed/15201626.

Hewlett, Sylvia Ann. *Executive Presence: The Missing Link Between Merit and Success*. New York: HarperCollins, 2014.

———. *Forget a Mentor. Find a Sponsor*. Boston, MA: Harvard Business Review Press, 2013.

Hochschild, Arlie, and Anne Machung. *The Second Shift: Working Families and the Revolution at Home*. New York: Penguin Group, 2012.

Hsieh, Tony. *Delivering Happiness: A Path to Profits, Passion, and Purpose*. New York: Business Plus, 2010.

Hunt, Vivian, Dennis Layton, and Sara Prince. *Diversity Matters*. McKinsey & Company. February 2, 2015. https://www.mckinsey .com/~/media/mckinsey/business%20functions/organization /our%20insights/why%20diversity%20matters/diversity%20matters .ashx.

Longman, Karen. "Sticky Floors? Stained Glass Ceilings? Addressing Barriers That Deter Women from Leadership." Breakout Sessions, Advancing Women in Leadership Conference. Azusa Pacific University. March 5, 2018.

Ludden, Jennifer. "Ask for a Raise? Most Women Hesitate." National Public Radio. February 8, 2011. https://www.npr.org/2011/02/14 /133599768/ask-for-a-raise-most-women-hesitate.

Martin, Peggy. *The Therapeutic Use of Self*. London, England: Palgrave, 1987.

McCloskey, Robert. US State Department spokesman recorded by Marvin Kalb, CBS reporter. *TV Guide*. March 31, 1984. Citing an unspecified press briefing during the Vietnam War.

McGinn, Kathleen L. and Nicole Tempest. "Heidi Roizen." Harvard Business School Case 800-228. January 2000. Last modified April 2010. https://www.hbs.edu/faculty/Pages/item.aspx?num=26880.

McGuire, Gail M. "Gender, Race, and the Shadow Structure: A Study of Informal Networks and Inequality in a Work Organization." *Gender and Society* 16, no. 3 (2002): 303–22. http://www.jstor.org /stable/3081781.

Mencken, Henry Louis. *Prejudices: Second Series*. New York: Alfred A. Knopf, 1920.

Meyer, Joseph. *The Search to Belong: Rethinking Intimacy, Community, and Small Groups*. Grand Rapids, MI: Zondervan, 2003.

Miller, Claire. "Unintended Consequences of Sexual Harassment Scandals." *New York Times*. October 9, 2017. https://www.nytimes.com/2017/10/09/upshot/as-sexual-harassment-scandals-spook-men-it-can-backfire-for-women.html. Accessed April 20, 2018.

Milne-Tyte, Ashley, host. Episode 105: "The Assistant." *The Broad Experience* (MP3 podcast). Posted on May 15, 2017. https://itunes.apple.com/us/podcast/the-broad-experience/id524835071?mt=2.

Mohair, Tara. "Why Women Don't Apply for Jobs Unless They're 100% Qualified." *Harvard Business Review*. August 24, 2014. https://hbr.org/2014/08/why-women-dont-apply-for-jobs-unless-theyre-100-qualified.

Palmer, Parker. *Let Your Life Speak: Listening for the Voice of Your Vocation*. San Francisco, CA: Jossey-Bass, 2000.

Payne, Keith, Laura Niemi, and John M. Doris. "How to Think About Implicit Bias." *Scientific American*. March 27, 2018. https://www.scientificamerican.com/article/how-to-think-about-implicit-bias/.

Pronin, Emily, Daniel Y. Lin, and Lee Ross. "The Bias Blind Spot: Perceptions of Bias in Self Versus Others." *Personality and Social Psychology Bulletin* 28, no. 3 (March 2002): 369–81. https://doi.org/10.1177/0146167202286008.

Rogers, Rod. *Pastor Driven Stewardship: 10 Steps to Lead Your Church to Biblical Giving*. Dallas, TX: Brown Books, 2006.

Roys, Julie (host). "What Is God's Vision for Womanhood?" *Up for Debate* (MP3 podcast). Moody Bible Radio. Posted December 9, 2017. https://moodyaudio.com/products/what-gods-vision-womanhood.

Ryrie, Charles. *Basic Theology*. Wheaton, IL: Victor Books, 1986.

Sandberg, Sheryl. *Lean In: Women, Work and the Will to Lead*. New York: Alfred A. Knopf, 2013.

Santhanam, Laura. "Poll: A Third of Women Say They've Been Sexually Harassed or Abused at Work." *PBS News Hour*. November 21, 2017.

https://www.pbs.org/newshour/nation/poll-a-third-of-women-say
-theyve-been-sexually-harassed-or-abused-at-work.

Scazzero, Peter. *The Emotionally Healthy Leader: How Transforming Your Inner Life Will Deeply Transform Your Church, Team, and the World.* Grand Rapids, MI: Zondervan, 2015.

Schleifer, Cyrus, and Amy D. Miller. "Occupational Gender Inequality Among American Clergy, 1976–2016: Revisiting the Stained-Glass Ceiling." *Sociology of Religion* 78, no. 4 (January 8, 2018): 387–410. https://doi.org/10.1093/socrel/srx032.

Schawbel, Dan. "Sylvia Ann Hewlett: Find a Sponsor Instead of a Mentor." *Forbes.* September 10, 2013. https://www.forbes.com/sites /danschawbel/2013/09/10/sylvia-ann-hewlett-find-a-sponsor-instead -of-a-mentor/#3f5aa1801760.

Scholer, David M. "1 Timothy 2:9–15 & The Place of Women in the Church's Ministry." In *Women, Authority & The Bible.* Edited by Alvera Michelsen. Downers Grove, IL: InterVarsity Press, 1986.

Shambaugh, Rebecca. *It's Not a Glass Ceiling, It's A Sticky Floor: Free Yourself from the Hidden Behaviors Sabotaging Your Career Success.* New York: McGraw-Hill Books, 2008.

Shellnut, Kate. "Women's March Sets Out to Exclude 40 Percent of American Women." *Christianity Today.* January 18, 2017. https:// www.christianitytoday.com/women/2017/january/womens-march -sets-out-to-exclude-40-percent-of-american-wom.html.

Smith, Efrem, Tara Beth Leach, David Fitch, and Juliet Liu. "Let Women Lead." Live Webinar, Missio Alliance, February 22, 2018. https:// www.missioalliance.org/product/let-women-lead-webinar/.

Stein, Steven J., and Howard E. Book. *The EQ Edge: Emotional Intelligence and Your Success.* Mississauga, ON: Jossey-Bass, 2006.

Strong, James. *The Strongest Strong's Exhuastive Concordance of the Bible.* Grand Rapids, MI: Zondervan, 2001.

Sweigart, Ann. "Women on Board for Change: The Norway Model of Boardroom Quotas as a Tool for Progress in the United States and Canada." *Northwest Journal of International Law & Business*, 32, no. 4 (2012): 81a. http://scholarlycommons.law.northwestern.edu/njilb/vol32/iss4/6.

The Sloan Center on Aging & Work at Boston College. "Employers Need: Improved Performance & Productivity." http://workplaceflexibility. bc.edu/need/need_employers_performance. Accessed May 25, 2018.

Thompson, Krissah. "In March on Washington, White Activists Were Largely Overlooked but Strategically Essential." *Washington Post.* August 25, 2013. https://www.washingtonpost.com/lifestyle/style /in-march-on-washington-white-activists-were-largely-overlooked -but-strategically-essential/2013/08/25/f2738c2a-eb27-11e2-8023 -b7f07811d98e_story.html?utm_term=.d975b97a5a9c.

Turner, Laura Ortberg. "The Christian F-Word." *Christianity Today.* September 25, 2013. https://www.christianitytoday.com /women/2013/september/christian-f-word.html.

U.S. Congregations. "What Are the Major Challenges That U.S. Congregations Face?" *USCLS* (U.S. Congregational Life Survey blog). http://www.uscongregations.org/blog/2014/02/17/what-are-the-major -challenges-that-u-s-congregations-face/. Accessed October 10, 2018.

Valerio, Anna Marie, and Kartina Sawyer. "The Men Who Mentor Women." *Harvard Business Review.* December 7, 2016. https://hbr.org /2016/12/the-men-who-mentor-women.

Vasel, Kathryn. "5 Things to Know About the Gender Pay Gap." CNN Money. April 4, 2017. http://money.cnn.com/2017/04/04/pf/equal -pay-day-gender-pay-gap/index.html?iid=EL.

Walker, Susan, J. Bastow Wilson, John B. Steel, G. L. Rapson, Benjamin Smith, Warren McG. King, and Yvette H. Cottam. "Properties of Ecotones: Evidence from Five Ecotones Objectively Determined from a Coastal Vegetation Gradient." *Journal of Vegetation Science* 14, no. 4 (April 9, 2009): 579–90. https://doi.org/10.1111/j.1654-1103.2003. tb02185.x.

Wilkerson, Robyn. *Shattering the Stained Glass Ceiling: A Coaching Strategy for Women Leaders in Ministry.* Springfield, MO: Influence Resources, 2017.

Williams, Joan. "What Works for Women at Work." Book event, Stanford, California. April 15, 2014. http://gender.stanford.edu /news/2014/what-works-women-work. Accessed March 22, 2018.

ABOUT THE AUTHOR

Kadi Cole is one of the most experienced authorities in organizational and leadership development in the church today. With a background in executive leadership at one of the largest multisite churches in America and a master's degree in human resource development, she offers practical strategies and insights that are relevant and easily applicable to present-day church culture.

Kadi helps individuals and teams uncover and fulfill their God-given purpose with more effectiveness and joy through her international work as an organizational consultant, leadership trainer, and LifePlan facilitator. As one of the first female leaders to serve in an executive role at a large, multisite church, Kadi is a founding member of the Women's Executive Pastor Network and also works with churches to create environments in which female leaders can be fully developed, thrive in their calling, and help fulfill the mission of their churches.

Kadi's tell-it-like-it-is attitude is a refreshing approach that allows her to authentically connect with those aspiring to go to their next level of leadership and impact.

Connect with Kadi at www.kadicole.com or on social media @kadicole.